THE
HBCU
EXPERIENCE

THE HBCU ROYAL UNIVERSITY QUEENS 2nd EDITION

Visionary Author: Dr. Ashley Little
Lead Author: Bridgett Herring Williams
Foreword Author: Dr. Judy Rashid
Foreword Author: Dr. Dale Williams

Published By: The HBCU Experience Movement, LLC

The HBCU Experience Movement, LLC

thehbcuexperiencemovement@gmail.com

Ordering Information:
Quantity Sales: Special discounts are available on quantity purchases by corporations, associations, and nonprofits. For details, contact the publisher at the address above.

ISBN: 978-1-7349311-7-4

DR. ASHLEY LITTLE

A Message from the Founder
Dr. Ashley Little

Historically Black Colleges & Universities (HBCUs) were established to serve the educational needs of black Americans. During the time of their establishment, and many years afterward, blacks were generally denied admission to traditionally white institutions. Prior to The Civil War, there was no structured higher education system for black students. Public policy, and certain statutory provisions, prohibited the education of blacks in various parts of the nation. Today, HBCUs represent a vital component of American higher education.

The HBCU Experience Movement, LLC is a collection of stories from prominent alumni throughout the world, who share how their HBCU experience molded them into the people they are today. We are also investing financially into HBCUs throughout the country. Our goal is to create a global movement of prominent HBCU alumni throughout the nation to continue to share their stories each year, allowing us to give back to prestigious HBCUs annually.

We are proud to present to you *The HBCU Experience: The HBCU Royal University Queens 2nd Edition*. We would like to acknowledge and give a special thanks to our amazing lead author/partner, Bridgett Herring Williams, for your dedication and commitment. We appreciate you and thank you for your hard work and dedication on behalf of this project. We would also like to give a special thanks to our foreword authors, expert authors, contributing authors and partners for believing in this movement and investing your time, and monetary donations, to give back to your school. We appreciate all of the The HBCU Royal University Queens who shared your HBCU Queen experience in this publication.

About Dr. Ashley Little

Dr. Ashley Little is The CEO/Founder of Ashley Little Enterprises, LLC which encompasses her Media, Consulting Work, Writing, Ghost Writing, Book Publishing, Book Coaching, Project Management, Magazine, Public Relations & Marketing, and Empowerment Speaking. In addition, she is an Award-Winning Serial Entrepreneur, TV/Radio Host, TEDx Speaker, International Speaker, Keynote Speaker, Media Maven, Journalist, Writer, Host, Philanthropist, Business Coach, Investor, Advisor for She Wins Society and 14X Award-Winning Best Selling Author. As seen on Black Enterprise(2X), Sheen Magazine (Print and Online), Sheen Talk, Voyage ATL, Fox Soul TV, NBC, Fox, CBS, BlackNews.Com, Shoutout Miami, Shoutout Atlanta, TEDx Speaker, Morning Star, Yahoo Finance, Heart and Soul, The Book of Sean, HBCU Times, VIP Global Magazine, The Black Report, Vocal, Ted.com, Medium, Soul Wealth, Hustle and Soul, BlackBusiness.com, New York WeeklyTop 10 Hardest Working CEOs alongside Billionaire Mark Cuban, US Insiders Top 10 Women Entrepreneurs alongside Billionaire and Media Mogul Oprah Winfrey, CEO Weekly Top 10 Influential People In 2021 alongside Billionaires Jeff Bezos and Beyonce' and many more. She is also a proud member of The Chancellors Round Table at North Carolina A&T State University.

She is a proud member of Delta Sigma Theta Sorority Incorporated, and a member of Alpha Phi Omega. She is very involved in her community, organizations and non-profits. Currently, she is the Co-Founder of Sweetheart Scholars Non-profit Organization 501 (C-3) along with three other powerful women. This scholarship is given out annually to African American Females from her hometown of Wadesboro, North Carolina who are attending college to help with their expenses. Dr. Little believes it takes a village to raise a child and to never forget where you come from. Dr. Little is a strong believer in giving back to her community. She believes our young ladies need vision, direction, and strong mentorship. She is the CEO/Founder/Visionary Author of The HBCU Experience Movement, LLC the first Black-owned company to launch books written and published by prominent alumni throughout the world who attended Historically Black Colleges & Universities. As authors, they share a powerful collection of stories on how their unique college experience has molded them into the people they are today. Our company's goal is to change the narrative by sharing Black stories and investing financially back into our HBCUs to increase young alumni giving and enrollment. The Award-Winning Best Selling Authors won the Black Authors Matter TV Award May 2021 and winner of the International Book Awards by The American Book Fest. The books are also apart of the WorldCat.Org the world's largest network of library content and services. Dr. Little is also the Editor and Chief of Creating Your Seat At The Table International Magazine, Advisor for She Wins Society, and Writing and Publishing Coach for the WILDE Winner's Circle.

She is the Founder and Owner of T.A.L.K Radio & TV Network, LLC. Airs in over 167 countries, streamed LIVE on Facebook, YouTube, Twitter and Periscope. Broadcasting and Media Production Company. This live entertainment platform is for new or existing radio shows, television shows, or other electronic media outlets, to air content from a centralized source. All news, information or music shared on this platform are solely the responsibility of the station/radio owner. She is also the Owner and Creator of Creative Broadcasting Radio Station the station of "unlimited possibilities" and Podcast, Radio/TV Host. She is also one of the hosts of the new TV Show Daytime Drama National Syndicated Television Show which will be aired on Comcast Channel 19 and ATT Channel 99 in 19 Middle Tennessee Counties. It will also air on The United Broadcasting Network, The Damascus Roads Broadcasting Network, and Roku.

She is CEO/Founder/Visionary Author of The HBCU Experience Movement LLC and CEO/Founder of Little Publishing LLC.

Dr. Little is a 14X Award-Winning Best Selling Author of "Dear Fear, Volume 2 18 Powerful Lessons Of Living Your Best Life Outside Of Fear", "The Gyrlfriend Code Volume 1", "I Survived", "Girl Get Up, and Win", "Glambitious Guide to Being An Entrepreneur", The Price of Greatness, The Making Of A Successful Business Woman, and "Hello Queen". She is a Co-Host for The Tamie Collins Markee Radio Show, Award-Winning Entrepreneur, Reflection Contributor for the book "NC Girls Living In A Maryland World, Sales/Marketing/Contributing Writer/Event Correspondent for SwagHer Magazine, Contributing Writer for MizCEO Magazine, Contributing Editor for SheIs Magazine, ContributingWriter/ National Sales Executive for Courageous Woman Magazine, Contributing Writer for Upwords International Magazine (India), Contributing Writer/Global Partner for Powerhouse Global International Magazine(London), Host of "Creating Your Seat At The Table", Host of "Authors On The Rise", Co-Host Glambitious Podcast, Partner/Visionary Author of The Gyrlfriend Code The Sorority Edition along with The Gyrlfriend Collective, LLC and CEO/Visionary Author of The HBCU Experience The North Carolina A&T State University Edition. She has been on many different Podcasts, TV Shows, Magazines, and Radio Shows. Lastly, she has received awards such as "Author Of The Month", The Executive Citation of Anne Arundel County, Maryland Award which was awarded by the County Executive Steuart L. Pittman, Top 28 Influential Business Pioneers for K.I.S.H Magazine Spring 2019 Edition. She has been featured in SwagHer Magazine, Power20Magazine Glambitious, Sheen Magazine, All About Inspire Magazine, Formidable Magazine, BRAG Magazine, Sheen Magazine, Front Cover of MizCEO Magazine November 2019, Front Cover for UpWords Magazine October 2019 Edition, Courageous Woman Magazine, Courageous Woman Special Speakers Edition November 2019, Influence Magazine,

Featured/Interviewed On a National Syndicated Television Show HBCU 101 on Aspire TV, Dynasty of Dreamers K.I.S.H Magazine Spring 2019 Edition, Dynasty of Dreamers K.I.S.H Magazine September 2019 Edition, Front Cover of Courageous Magazine December 2019, Front Cover of Doz International Magazine January 2020, Top 28 Influential Business Pioneers for K.I.S.H Magazine, Power20 Magazine Glambitious January 2020, Power20 Magazine Glambitious February 2020, Featured in Powerhouse Global International London Magazine March 2020 edition, Featured in National Boss Magazine October 2020 Edition, Featured in Sheen Magazine February 2020 as one of "The Top 20 Women To Be On The Lookout For In 2020, BlackNews.com, BlackBusiness.com, Front Cover She Speaks Magazine August 2020, Front Cover National Boss Magazine November 2020, BlackNewsScoop.com, Awarded National Women's Empowerment Ministry "Young, Gifted, & Black Award" February 2020 which honors and celebrate women in business such as Senior Level Executives, Entrepreneurs and CEO's below age 40 for their creativity and business development. Featured in National Women Empowerment Magazine 2020, Featured in Black Enterprise 2020, Featured on Fox, NBC, CBS 2020, Featured/Interviewed on National Syndicated Television The Black Report on Fox Soul TV, Front Cover for National Boss Magazine 2020, Speaker at The Black College Expo 2020, Speaker for Creative CEO's summit January 2021, International Speaker for Living Your Dream Life Summit 2021, Speaker for Elite Business Women Powershift Conference 2021, Keynote Speaker/Host/Panelist for The Bella, The Brand & Her Bag Wealth Summit 2021, Speaker for The Unstoppable You Summit January 2021, Speaker for Marketing Mastery Summit for Glambitious 2021, Speaker for Crown Yourself Conference January 2021, Featured in Sheen Print Magazine 2021, Speaker at Door Dash Virtual Black History Month Celebration, Speaker for Day Of Aggie Generations with North Carolina A&T State University, 2021 Woman of Black Excellence Honoree, Guest/Speaker on podcast The Happy Hour Show, Speaker for the Phoenix Jack & Jill HBCU Author Showcase, Guest/Speaker on The JMosley Show, Contributing Author for "Prayers For The Entrepreneurial Woman Book", Speaker for Creative Con, Recognized as one of Today's Black History Makers, Speaker at From Paper to Profits conference, Press Conference/Press for "Don't Waste Your Petty" Movie, Press Conference/Press for Mahalia Jackson movie, Speaker for HerStory Women's Global Empowerment Summit, Speaker for HerStory Women Who Lead Conference, Speaker for Stepping N2 Sisterhood Sharing Winning Secrets Virtual Summit, Speaker for I AM Glambitious Virtual Conference, Speaker for Black Authors Matter TV show, Speaker for Thought Leaders Global Virtual Summit, Speaker for A Conversation with Floyd Marshall Jr., Black Authors Matter TV Award Winner, Speaker for Sheen Talk, Foreword Author for the anthology "It Cost To Be The Boss", Top 50 Most Influential Women recognized by VIP Global Magazine, Speaker at Black Writers Weekend, Speaker on The GameChangers With Angela Ward Show Keynote Speaker for Blacks In Nonprofits Conference, Speaker for Leap Conference, Speaker on Pass The Mic Sis, Speaker for From Purpose to Profit Summit, Speaker on The Been Worthy Podcast as well to name a few.

Dr. Little received her undergraduate degree in English from North Carolina A&T State University. Next, she received her Master's Degree in Industrial Organizational Psychology. She has received her Doctorate in Humanitarian and Leadership as well. Dr. Little is a mover and shaker and she continuously pushes herself to be better than she was yesterday. She gives GOD all the credit for everything that has happened in her life. She has strong faith and determination to be great. She believes her only competition is herself. Her favorite scripture is Philippians 4:13 "I can do all things through Christ who strengthens me".

Table of Contents

continued...

DR. JUDY NAZIRAH RASHID

Foreword
Dr. Judy Nazirah Rashid
Advisor to Miss A&T 1990-2010

On November 30, 1974 there appeared a strange fossil, which was determined to be three and half million years old, in the Olduvai Gorge in Northern, Tanzania. Olduvai Gorge is a site that holds the earliest evidence of the existence of human ancestors. Paleoanthropologists have found hundreds of fossilized bones and stone tools in the area dating back millions of years, leading them to conclude that humans evolved in Africa. (https://www.livescience. com/40455-olduvai-gorge.html) The fossil, found by paleontologists, was the remains of an African woman whom they affectionately named LUCY. History has since recorded, and as cited by Simone Schwarz –Bart in her book In Praise of Black Women- Ancient African Queens, that *Lucy is the grandmother to us all, blacks and whites, yellows, reds, people of the sea and dwellers of the steppe, those who live with the sun or with the polar cold.* She is undisputed as the one womb from which all of humanity came.

Help me salute Mother Queen Lucy, also known as Black Eve, and all of her daughters, the Queens of Historically Black Colleges and Universities of the 20th and 21st century. They honor those who came before them and lead generations forward. They are poised, spiritual, intelligent, caring, and beautiful. They are courageous, and daring as they lead. They are honorable yet wear their titles humbly for life as they serve the people who made them queen. They are the voice for the voiceless and have hope for the hopeless. They are the sum total of womanhood at its finest. Once a queen, always a queen. Listen to their stories; be inspired to serve.

Written by Dr. Judy Rashid
University Queen Advisor, 1991-2011

About Dr. Judy Nazirah Rashid

Dr. Judy Nazirah Rashid is Founder and CEO of Skills Training and Development Consulting Services (STADCS). She has been involved in education for the last 44 years as teacher and school principal (K-12), senior student affairs administrator, and as adjunct faculty in Liberal Studies (Conflict Resolution) and the PhD Program in Leadership Studies. As the Associate Vice Chancellor for Student Affairs, she supervised Student Conduct, International Students, Veterans and Student Disability Support Services, Multicultural Students, Greek Life, and Student Government where she also supervised the University Queens for 20 years.

She recently retired as the Associate Vice Chancellor for Student Affairs / Dean of Students from her undergraduate alma mater, North Carolina A&T State University. Currently she serves as an Adjunct Assistant Professor in the Dept. of Adult Education and Leadership Studies.

Since 1989, Dr. Rashid has been professionally involved in conflict management education and training including international conflict resolution in South Africa. For almost two decades, she has garnered financial educational support for South African youth and adults. In December 2019, a recently erected building in Vanderjilpark, South Africa was name the Dr. Judy Rashid Education and Leadership Center.

Dr. Rashid received her Bachelor of Science and Masters' degrees (both summa cum laude) from North Carolina A&T and her doctoral degree in higher education administration from North Carolina State University in Raleigh. She holds certification in both interaction management and performance management from the State of North Carolina, advanced training in teaching negotiation in the organization from Harvard University, complete course training in N.C. Law for Non-Attorney Mediators, Mediation Certification Training/N.C. Superior Court Mediated Settlement Conferences, and Mediation Certification Training/Equal Employment Opportunity Commission.

Dr. Rashid is a member of the N.C. Bar Association (Dispute Resolution Section) and the NC Association of Retired Governmental Employees. Dr. Rashid dedicates her civic life through service to the less fortunate and is a Charter Member of both the National Museum of African American History and Culture of Washington D.C. and of the International African American Museum in Charleston, S.C.

Dr. Rashid is married and has two adult sons and an outstanding grandson.

DR. DALE WILLIAMS

Foreword

Dr. Dale Williams

Miss Tennessee State University 1992-1993

Leadership For Queens, Founder

The idea of being a college queen for many young women seems like a dream come true, but for many of the writers in this book it has been a life-changing reality that has shaped them into the women they are today. Nothing is more exhilarating than for a young African American female to be honored by her peers and University for her ability to lead as an official student spokesperson. Upon winning, she becomes a part of history that is embedded in African American tradition forever.

Being an HBCU college queen is a time-honored tradition I will never forget. Through years of research, I have learned that these positions are uniquely different from any other "Miss" title in existence. As you read these personal accounts in this book, you will get an inside look at life changing moments when some African American women have gained acceptance, love, and confidence, while others experienced growth, learned lessons, and received opportunities, but with each reign, a queen emerged. Not the queen that comes because you won the title, but the queen that connects you to something bigger than yourself. It is at this point that one realizes just how these positions evolve and speak to the pride and tradition of HBCU colleges and universities, thus highlighting their mission to develop not just the mind but the whole person. These colleges and universities saw fit to place honor on African American women not only for their beauty, but also for their academic accomplishments and leadership skills. Yet accomplishments and leadership have never been an issue for African American women, as we have excelled in so many areas. Still, many will say they struggle to see themselves as beautiful.

Our young women need to understand that they are beautiful though the world counters our beauty and sublimely chips away at our self-esteem. Who can forget the 2011 *Psychology Today* article by psychologist Satoshi Kanazawa titled "Why Are Black Women Less Physically Attractive Than Other Women?" Although the article was met with outrage, the reality is black women are the least represented in our versatility in a beautiful way. Thus, when I became a black college queen for the first time, I felt represented. HBCUs created the position of campus queen to uplift black women because the world sometimes placed us under its feet. However, on HBCU campuses, the queen is special and honored by her community. HBCU queens can be traced to the 1920s when these college and universities found themselves emphasizing new images of black people, and black women were no exception. The creation of the HBCU queen gave African Americans the ability to create their own image of beauty. By the 1970s, thanks to *Ebony* magazine's annual spotlight of campus queens, just about every HBCU college and university had an African-American female to represent their campus. Today HBCU queens serve their institutions in various ways as spokespersons, recruiters, and leaders. Many serve as a beacon of hope to young impressionable minds wanting to go to college, as well as role models, mentors, and leaders to their peers. Each queen can attest to witnessing the glimmer in a little girl's eye when she has encountered the presence of an HBCU queen because we know for the first time, she sees herself.

While each HBCU campus has created their own model and standard of what it means to be "queen," we can all agree that she will always be a part of African American history and culture. I am not aware of any other program that has fully represented the African American female as a whole, focusing on our best attributes externally and internally. Consequently, we must never forget the HBCU queen and the contributions she has made, what she represents, or negate her experiences. Her unique historical position is just as important now as it was then. In a world that devalues black women and coins us at times in the most negative ways, these leadership positions remind young women of the importance of their worth. HBCUs saw the queen in us, and for that we will be forever grateful. This is our story. This is the *HBCU Royal University Queens Edition.*

To Be a Queen

You know I try to make people understand

It's not the way I wave my hand

It's not the things I do or say

It's not my walk, lean or sway

It's just the little things in me

that let me know that

I'm a queen

To be a queen

I am a queen

In my heart.

It's not the crown that I wore

Or the title that I bore

It's just what I choose to do

Because of my love for my HBCU

To be a queen

I am their queen

In my heart.

–Dale-licately said

Dale Williams is the founder of Leadership for Queens, host of HBCU Kings and Queens Conference, and served as Miss Tennessee State University 1992-1993.

About Dr. Dale Michelle Williams

Dale Williams is the founder of Leadership for Queens, a leadership conference for Historically Black University and College (HBCU) Queens. She has organized and conducted the conference annually for HBCU queens and kings for 19 years. She has more than 20 years of experience in higher education. Currently, Dale is an academic advisor at University of Memphis as well as an instructor at Bethel University. She is a sought after trainer and speaker that has also worked at many HBCU's in a variety of capacities. Dale's leadership aspirations began early as she was not only queen of her high school (Hamilton) in Memphis, TN, but also Miss Tennessee State University (TSU) 1992-93. Dale has judged and worked with various pageants, served as a motivational keynote speaker and conducted numerous leadership workshops at various universities, conferences and community events. She believes that those who walk in such positions as the HBCU king or queen have the perfect opportunity to make a great impact on others. Dale is a member of community/public service organizations such as Delta Sigma Theta Sorority, Inc., Junior League of Memphis and TSU Alumni Association. She received a Bachelor of Science degree in Speech Communications and Theatre and a Master's of Arts in English from Tennessee State University. She has a graduate certificate in African-American Literature from University of Memphis. She thoroughly enjoys helping young men and women reach their goals and realize their full potential. She enjoys giving back to her community.

BRIDGETT HERRING WILLIAMS

The Bracelet

Bridgett Herring Williams

Miss North Carolina A&T State University 1997-1998

I couldn't stop crying. Lying hopelessly defeated in the fetal position on the office floor of my advisor, I was … *crying. Hysterically crying.* In this moment, I was inconsolable. This was so far from the composure of my character. Still, this time, I couldn't hold back the dam of tears that poured relentlessly down my face and neck as each breath flooded my heart with overwhelming anxiety. I was in disbelief. This simply could not be happening. This couldn't be true. I'd worked meticulously every day for months. Now, this! I didn't want to disappoint anyone. I had so much riding on this. Everything had to be perfect. I had to be perfect because, after all, all eyes would be on me, the *queen*.

I was *Miss A&T* 1997-1998.

I will never forget the day I was crowned Miss A&T. It was Thursday, October 23, 1997. Although I was crowned at a coronation ceremony later that evening, I had already *become* Miss A&T. My ascension began after a breakdown. A breakdown that landed me on the floor, sobbing in front of my advisor, whom I always went to when I needed sound advice and had challenges. Upon composing myself, I explained my uncommon hysteria to her. I explained that the purchase order for the bracelets I wanted for my court and myself had not been submitted. After staying up all night to make sure Corbett Sports Center was going to look perfect for the queen's coronation that evening, all the rehearsals, the dress fittings, and no drama between the young ladies on my court, we were not going to have bracelets.

This was not happening. The perfect day, the day I had worked all summer to plan, was going to be ruined over *bracelets*. I know you read "bracelets" and you may be asking, "Are you serious? You were on the floor hyperventilating over jewelry?" To that I say, "Yes," but "No." It wasn't about the bracelets from a material sense, but rather what the bracelets represented. They represented *respect*.

It was my junior year, and I had a strong desire to create a mentoring program for girls at a local middle school in Greensboro, North Carolina. There was already a program for the boys in place; however, nothing had been established for the girls. My desire was to create a mentoring relationship that would allow young black girls to see and connect with positive, ambitious examples of themselves in everyday society. I wanted to do that through counsel and interaction with my peers and myself. I have a passion for serving young people, especially young ladies. That is what was taught to me. It is the legacy of mentorship and counsel that I learned from the matriarchs in my life, including my mother, Mariam; my grandmothers, Alice and Ruth; my aunts, Portia and Patricia; and my Godmother, Della. Making them proud meant that I should be authentically me, understanding that being a queen is not a one-size-fits-all crown.

I was the heir to the throne. I was the legacy of all my sister queens. But before them, I was the legacy of the queens who raised me. They taught me the "black girl magic" of being in the front and the back at the same time; that is, leading from the frontline while providing encouragement and support from the back. A queen embraces all that she is and she does not conform to what others may project upon her. She listens to wise counsel around her and humbly accepts advice. A queen looks out for others with an open heart while challenging herself, and those around her, to produce the best version of themselves.

I was taught a culture of sisterhood, strength and self-pride. I wanted to share this mantra in my new mentoring program, Aggie Q.U.E.E.N.S. These young ladies would exhibit Quality, Understanding and Enrichment through Education, Nurturing and

Success. This was the motivating factor in me deciding to run for Miss A&T. The respect associated with the position would turn up the volume of my voice and help influence greater change. Therefore, it became my mission to operate in excellence and to operate in perfection—as a leader, as a professional and as a young black woman. I wanted to leave no room for doubt so there was absolutely no room for error. Perfection equated to control and control garnered respect.

So regarding the bracelet, it was never about the jewelry. It was about the perfect presentation of an expectation. An expectation–I created for myself where I had to be the perfect representative of my peers. I arrived at meetings and events on time, wearing all the right things, saying all the right things, and making all the right community connections to push my platform forward as a responsible student. Yet and still, on this day, in that moment, I realized that no matter how hard I tried, I would never be *perfect*. I had to break out of those narrow expectations. That need to be perfect. By default, that had me feeling like a failure. I felt like a failure for not meeting expectations, which was also my biggest fear.

Ironically, on the day that I was to be crowned Miss A&T, I was still being mentored by my advisor, just as much as the middle school girls I had come to mentor. My advisor listened to me with a calm ear. She encouraged me and helped me resolve the issue by contacting a former queen, who stepped in to provide the bracelets. The network of sisterhood and support that I have received from my experiences as an HBCU Queen has been an invaluable tool and asset in my journey and approach to mentoring. Being able to inner-stand and identify with girls of our culture allows me to relate just how we all have our own bracelet story.

Your bracelets, unlike mine, may not have been living up to a certain expectation. Your bracelet may be colorism, anxiety, feelings of inadequacy, bravery, financial issues, educational challenges and more. The list goes on and on for the personal challenges one may face. As an African-American, it is evident that we all feel we have to work harder or prove ourselves just for status quo. But there is also the game *within the game* that *black women* encounter. You have to work even harder to prove that you're smarter than the intellect of men's pride. You know the feeling that you must be "superwoman" to everyone around you. For me, on that particular day, it was a minor expectation that I assigned a major role to. It was a box of perfection, an image that I had to maintain for respect. After all, part of knowing the role is looking the part. Right?

I guess it all depends on the character you play. Are you playing a role true to the audience in your life, or is it true to the audience within yourself? I can answer for me. Attending an HBCU taught me that I do not have to play a character. Too often this is the stigma perpetuated and placed on African-Americans, especially black women. We must fit into a mold or box to keep the peace and not incite insecurity within the system of patriarchal pride. No. This is not my truth. I simply have to educate myself about myself and be what I am. *Queen.* And, as a queen representing an HBCU, you understand that queens are diverse. They have different hair. Some wear makeup while others wear no makeup. They have different beliefs and they come in different shades. I learned that being a true queen is not about your title. Instead, it's about your nature. A crown does not dictate a queen. It's not about the jewels that you put on to adorn yourself. Instead, it's about the jewels you develop within.

Attending an HBCU has the great benefit of allowing one to discover themselves in a familiar community, while also establishing and building pride in a culturally safe environment. During that year, I learned to intertwine my greatness with the haunting of my flaws. That one year inevitably changed my life forever. My HBCU was undoubtedly important to me, and to represent her was one of the greatest honors I have ever had. Being Miss A&T taught me so much about myself. I am still a *queen.*

It took me a long time to accept myself for who I am, for my flaws and successes. I have discovered and nurtured the woman within me. My passion continues to evolve with my growth, and I continue to uplift our young black women in today's atmosphere of individuality and acceptance. I am more than any bracelet I could ever wear. The true beauty of a queen is her character. The value within that cannot be contained. You've heard it before. Tiara: $450. Gown and shoes: $2,500. Jewelry: $250. Heart of a Queen – *Priceless*.

I hope you enjoy the priceless stories of joy and triumph each of my Sister Queens share.

About Bridgett Herring Williams

Bridgett Herring Williams received her undergraduate degree in Construction Management from North Carolina A&T State University and a Master's in Public Administration from High Point University.

While a student at A&T, Bridgett was an active student leader, serving in many capacities and represented her alma mater as Miss North Carolina A&T State University, 1997-98. Upon graduation from college, Bridgett began a career in construction as an assistant project manager while also pursuing her passion for inner city youth, by volunteering for the local Boys and Girls Club. Thru her volunteerism, Bridgett learned more about the non-profit sector which eventually led to her career change. Dedicating almost 20 years to the non-profit sector, Bridgett has vast experiences as a program director to an executive director. Her demonstrated expertise has been in program development, grant writing, facilitating partnerships, consulting, and leading fundraising campaigns for non-profits of various sizes and missions. Working with the Boys & Girls Clubs of America, YMCA, Boy Scouts of America and the Marilyn G. Rabb Foundation, Bridgett learned the challenges of non-profit leadership from many different points of view. Additionally, she facilitates leadership development and management seminars and workshops for other community and faith based organizations. Having returned to her roots, Bridgett is currently the Director of Development for the College of Science & Technology at A&T and the Vice President of Albri Logistics, a transportation business she co-owns with her husband.

Bridgett is certain her primary purpose in life is to serve young people, most especially young women. She has served on several boards and held committee leadership positions within community organizations including Friends of Macedonia, JAL3 Ministries, Goodwill Industries, Project Potential, Cabarrus Charter Academy, Next Generation-The Movement, Charlotte-Mecklenburg Schools, Homeless Shelter Network and Keep Mecklenburg Beautiful. Her volunteer service has also expanded internationally with Samaritan's Feet in White River, South Africa.

She is a member of Delta Sigma Theta Sorority, Inc., National Council for Negro Women, the National Association of Women Professionals, Queen City Alumni Chapter of North Carolina A&T State University, the advisory board of 1,2,3 JUMP and serves as a consultant for several brands in the fashion and entertainment industry as well as non-profit organizations. Bridgett is a contributing author in 'The HBCU Experience Anthology-The North Carolina A&T State University Edition'.

Though her life serving the community is fulfilling, her greatest joy comes in spending time with her husband and daughter.

AYANNA SPIVEY

The Prototype

Ayanna Spivey

Miss Southern University and A&M 2013-2014

Being an HBCU campus queen has been defined by many as a "vanity title" or a "popularity contest". Some may call them a mascot of sorts. Though in some instances this can be true, the tradition of HBCU queens date back to the early 1900s. Just like most Black American traditions, we had to make a space for ourselves to celebrate ourselves. Black women weren't allowed to compete in the beauty pageants that were already established; therefore, a pageant was created their own for their own communities. This practice spread to HBCUs, starting with homecoming queens and then college queens reigning for the entirety of the academic year. Since then, the HBCU queen title along with their royal court has grown to represent the legacy, charity, and history of our treasured HBCUs. The most astonishing thing—that I still can't believe—is being a part of such a legacy as the 83rd Miss Southern University and A&M College.

My first introduction to an HBCU queen was the movie *School Daze*. The coronation scene made the role of being queen look so elaborate and grand, that I didn't want any parts of it. I was a clumsy tomboy who was rarely ever caught in skirts and dresses. Sashes and tiaras couldn't have been further from my interests. All of that changed once I arrived on The Bluff.

Meeting the current Miss Southern University and other Southwest Atlantic Conference (SWAC) queens while traveling during football season, changed my perspective. I saw myself in these women and aspired to accomplish some of the things they did like joining a sorority, excelling in their majors, and leaving a legacy on their institutions. This piqued my interests far more than watching Spike Lee's "Miss Mission College" who didn't have any speaking parts. Still veering away from any queen title, I desired to be a student leader like they were. I decided that I would find a role or position that would best suit me going into my sophomore year. After finding out many of friends were running for president and vice president positions, I didn't want to run against any of them. All that was left was the position of "Miss Sophomore". After some encouragement from my friends, I took a leap out my comfort zone and campaigned. Thankfully, I was successful in obtaining the title of Miss Sophomore during the 2011-2012 school year.

That same year I also became a member of the Alpha Tau Chapter of Delta Sigma Theta Sorority, Inc. I realized during that time, tiaras and sashes weren't all that bad; in fact, I may have even enjoyed it a little bit. These experiences also confirmed that being yourself goes a long way and that there is a place and time for everything. I learned that being a class queen and on the royal court can truly have a positive impact on the culture of the university during their reigns. With more college experiences and organizational involvements to follow as I matriculated into my junior year, becoming Miss Southern University no longer felt so foreign.

I've deemed my journey of becoming Miss Southern as the royal alignment. Every person I met up until that time, my sorority sisters, and family made this experience an unforgettable one and seemingly stress-free. I ran on the theme "The Prototype." According to Merriam-Webster, prototype is defined as "an original model on which something is patterned. My reign was just that—full of firsts that would have a lasting effect on the title and endeavors of the position. I wanted to accomplish two major things while being Miss Southern: to raise awareness and funds for agencies that support sickle cell and kidney disease, as well as elevate Southern University's notoriety even higher. Little did I know how these two goals would manifest themselves.

Sickle cell and kidney disease were important for me to bring awareness to and raise money for because they were two diseases that are highly prevalent in the Black community. My mother, at the time, had a rare kidney disease. As a result, she was on dialysis awaiting a kidney transplant Traditionally Miss Southerns raised money for "Up Til' Dawn," the nationwide college student-led organization that raises money for St. Jude's Children's Hospital. Every event Miss Southern or her court hosted, they would collect donations for that organization, and I had every intention to continue that tradition.

Unfortunately, soon after winning, I was contacted by a representative that we could no longer use the organization's name. From there, I met with my executive board, and we bounced ideas off of each other until we came up with another name—C.O.P.S. was born, which stands for Community Outreach Program Services. The goal of this new initiative was to allow myself and future Miss Southerns to pick any philanthropic cause they wanted to support. It took some time to get the campus on board and familiar with this new name as they were so accustomed to the former. Through the diligence of my court and C.O.P.S team we were able to raise $4,000, granting the Baton Rouge Sickle Cell Foundation and Baton Rouge Kidney Foundation $2,000 each.

The other goal was to elevate the Southern University name and its rich culture. Being from California, I realized there are no HBCUs there. You rarely ever hear much about them; and if you do, it's usually Morehouse, Spelman, or Howard. Southern is way better than those universities and I was determined to show others just why. My escort, Shaquille Dillon, and I decided to use my campaign's Instagram page as the official royal court page. Attending the NASAP Student Leadership Institute really assisted in helping that page grow. That was Southern's first time attending that conference in about ten years. Using the network gained from that conference and the usage of social media, Southern gained attention from those who may have not known much about the school. Following NASAP, I was informed by my advisor that a representative from the McDonald's 365Black Awards, asked for me to serve as that year's trophy girl. Also, our gospel choir was selected to sing behind gospel recording artist Erica Campbell. The highlight of the experience was giving Gladys Knight her lifetime achievement award. This was a major feat to promote our college and choir, as that awards show would air on BET that August. Things were coming together nicely, and the fall semester had not started yet.

As my reign was off to a great start, more and more opportunities came my way that surrounded press and media for the university. Many of which came from the Office of Communications. I was asked by one of the staff to participate in one of the commercials along with the Chancellor and other students. That experience led to do another commercial that I got to star in. This commercial not only aired locally throughout that year but it also aired during the Bayou Classic and SWAC championship games that were televised on NBC and ESPN. Another major feat accomplished that year was being featured on the front page of Sunday issue of The Advocate, the major newspaper outlet for Baton Rouge and its surrounding areas. This was especially significant because it was also the issue following our homecoming week along with LSU's homecoming. As most know news outlets historically tend to put HBCU's to the background especially when it is competing with other PWIs nearby. That was great year for media and Southern University especially going into the celebration the centennial year of Southern University relocating to Baton Rouge.

Being a Southern California native, it was always important to me to go back to my hometown of Moreno Valley to visit my high school and middle school to talk about the importance of HBCUs and college going overall. Due to my experiences, it became routine during my breaks from Southern to be solicited by former advisors, teachers, and church members to speak to students and youth groups. This opportunity expanded when my mother came up with the idea to come back home for the Black College Expo in Los Angeles to assist the LA alumni chapter and admissions with recruiting. It was a full circle moment when I realized that I was accepted to three HBCUs at that same expo three years prior.

The culmination of all of these experiences led to one last goal: competing for the Top 10 *Ebony* Campus Queens. Traditionally, *Ebony* Magazine would feature every HBCU queen along with highlighting HBCUs in their back-to-school issue that usually released every September. In 2010, they decided to move into a different direction with a competition where supporters for each school would vote to place their respective queens to be featured in *Ebony* magazine. Then the top 10 winners would go on to do an all-expense paid photoshoot in the city of the magazine's choice. I followed the competition over the years while in college and thought why wasn't Southern included. I did my research and found out only one other Miss Southern entered the competition and I contacted her to get some insight. The beginning of the school year I expressed to my advisor and my good friend, who was a photographer and videographer, that I wanted to participate. I asked him to keep any photos and videos he would take of me or of any events I hosted throughout the year for them to be included in the competition video. Through the support of the student services administration, the student body, family, friends, and supporters of Southern University, I was able to become a part of the 2014 Top 10 Campus Queens. The first Miss Southern to be featured since the competition's inception. This gave Southern University another opportunity to be featured on a national platform and since then 3 more Miss Southern's have been featured.

Though I came into Southern University with no intention of becoming a campus queen it was a journey like no other. I learned to adapt and adjust when things were out of my control like almost missing the Ebony shoot, and the bump in the road with St. Jude's. My self-confidence improved through the influx of requests to speak and attend various events. Participating in numerous committees that would assist in the selection of administration, homecoming, and centennial events, provided insight on all of the work that goes into the overall operation of a functioning institution. Thus, ultimately led to me pursuing a career in higher education. I saw how the students can play a major part in the recruiting and retention of their peers in promoting school spirit and advocacy. This experience specifically heightened my sense of responsibility to give back to my community and university. It was key in the development of my nonprofit, We Are Educated, Incorporated. The organization raises funds to assist students attending HBCUs as well as promote higher education at HBCUs and the legacy and impact of these institutions. The organization has given about $3000 since its inception and plans to increase its given as it is now a tax-exempt organization. Lastly, being Miss Southern allowed me to fully understand that being myself was and still is enough. I did not achieve all of these amazing things for the accolades, nor did I even pursue many of them. Life has a way of making a way for you when you step out on faith with your best foot forward. I am grateful to have been a part of this Southern University and HBCU legacy, for it has impacted my life and allowed me opportunities that I could have never imagined. To any future class and campus queens: being yourself should always be the theme to your campaign and the reign.

About Ayanna Spivey

Ayanna Spivey was born in the shadow of Southern University in Baton Rouge, LA. She was raised in Moreno Valley, Ca. Ayanna's leadership skills and creativity revealed themselves early in her childhood from being involved in her home church's youth ministry, youth choir, youth council, and various social events. She really explored those skills while in high school lettering in 3 sports, active in Associated Student Body, Black Student Union, and the becoming the Southern California Regional President of Black Student Unions. These experiences laid the foundation for her time at Southern University and the beginning of her career in higher education, through various positions in the Student Government Association, Miss Sophomore and then Miss Southern on the Royal Court. She also took part in the new student summer orientations, football recruiting, and being a member of the Alpha Tau chapter of Delta Sigma Theta Sorority Inc. All these endeavors sparked the ideas of wanting to go into higher education. Upon graduating from Southern University with a Bachelors Degree in Interdisciplinary Studies, with a concentration in Social Work and Sociology, she returned to California and received a Master of Science in Higher Education leadership and Student Development from California Baptist University.

With the culmination of her secondary and post-secondary education, in 2016 she launched We Are Educated, LLC. We Are Educated, LLC is an organization that strives to promote higher learning at HBCUs and inspire academic excellence through college preparation. It is the organization's belief that it can play a part in the increase of HBCU attendance by highlighting the benefits of the overall HBCU experience. We Are Educated, LLC provided scholarships to assist undergraduate students with their matriculation through various workshops and fairs. We Are Educated, LLC has provided about $3000 plus in giving within its first two years. We Are Educated, LLC, has now reorganized to We Are Educated, Incorporated a nonprofit tax exempt company.

Since her career path continued in California, Ayanna has worked within the California Community College system for seven years working with various programs that includes academic counseling, student services, academic success programs and with the California Department of Corrections and Rehabilitation. Her passions for equity and student success are evident in the work that she does within her perspective departments by always putting the students and their interests first. It is her hope to continue within the community college system while also contemplating on the idea of pursuing a doctoral degree. In the meantime, she continues to be active with the Southern University Alumni Federation Alumni Los Angeles Chapter, Southern University Young Alumni Network and she was named as one of SU's 40 Under Forty for the Inaugural Cohort in 2018.

SHAKARA PARKS

How Being a Queen of Morris College Molded Me into the Woman I am Today

Shakara Parks

Miss Morris College 2009-2010

Most little girls are nicknamed "Daddy's little princess" or just "Princess." Our definition of a princess is the daughter of a king and queen; but how many of us look at our parents in this nature? Yet, it has been instilled in us that we are or will be strong black women—black queens.

Black women have had an important role in forming our society as it is. A strong black woman, better known as a "queen," is proud of herself. Furthermore, she uses her accomplishments to inspire and encourage other women, especially within the black community. After losing loved ones or when going through tough times, I've realized that we tend to hold back our emotions to avoid showing weakness. As black women, we expose ourselves as strong and independent—queens.

Competing for Miss Morris was of high standards for me and it's another piece to my success story. The typical black HBCU queen is about empowering, mentoring, motivating and taking action to protect her campus, by any means necessary. An HBCU queen represents her alma mater to its fullest capacity. I will always and forever introduce myself as a former Miss Morris College because it's a part of who I am—an intelligent, successful, natural-born leader with a strong influence. In this chapter, I will share how being an HBCU queen molded me into the woman I am today.

I thought I would never compete for a title ever again after losing in the Miss Timberland Pageant in 2005 at my high school alma mater. Now that I think back to that night, I felt extremely low—not because I did not win, but because of all the hard work I put in. It was only five of us who competed, and I did not get anything. Not even a certificate of appreciation.

"What's next, Shakara? You are a natural born leader and a queen; do not give up!" Those were the words my mom told me on our way home after the pageant and coronation. Those words stuck with me until I got to college.

During my freshman year at Morris College, my group leader, former queen Iashea Simmons, was the reigning Miss Morris College. She was—and still is—a person who will build you back up and pour her energy into you. If it were not for her and the example she set, I would have never had the courage to compete for another title and run for Miss Morris College.

In April of 2009, flyers advertising the upcoming Miss Morris College went up around campus. I called my mom instantly to ask if I should compete in the pageant.

"Yes!" my mom exclaimed, of course. Before I knew it, my family came together to help with my campaign. After two weeks of campaigning, "It's Time for Nunu," which included hanging posters, spirit-driven activities, a specialized mixtape by a local DJ with an intro like no other, and a speech before the entire student body, the moment I had been anticipating and waiting for had finally arrived. I, Ms. Shakara Theirse, was crowned the 2009-2010 Miss Morris College.

While reigning as Miss Morris, I learned to treat myself like the queen my mom always told me I was. Being a queen allowed me to love myself more with much more confidence. This moment in my life made me feel like more than just a queen, but a woman who did not allow a past loss to dictate her future and purpose. After my coronation, "A Night of Enchantment and Divine Inspirations," a fire re-ignited inside of me. My goal was to use my life and my experiences as an example. I always knew deep down that I wanted to pour into the lives of young girls in such a way that others, such as Iashea Simmons a former queen, had poured into me.

One such opportunity came four years later when I was hired to choreograph the very pageant that I lost at my high school alma mater, Timberland High School. At first, I wondered if it would be a good idea to choreograph the pageant. I thought, "What would people think of me since I lost and now would be choreographing?" Thankfully, I stopped listening to that voice in my head, placed all those self-doubting thoughts aside and allowed God's voice to lead me.

True to His word, God turned my so-called failure into endless opportunities. Not only did I choreograph the Miss Timberland pageant, but I also became choreographer and pageant coach for local K-12 schools, Miss Black & Gold Pageants, Delta Sigma Theta, Inc. Cotillions, Miss Morris College Coronations, and much more. My career as a choreographer began to take off, and I always look back on my high school defeat and future win as Miss Morris as the two major impacts in my life. Had I never experienced what I thought was a devasting loss, I would have never tapped into the destiny God had for my life. None of my experiences thus far have been a waste. Being a queen has molded me into the business owner, pageant coach, and mentor I am today.

I want to leave this with anyone who ever thought about giving up after a loss: Sometimes, our lives are set up like a GPS. We set our destination to the place we would like to go, but what we do not realize is that there may be roadblocks, red lights, stop signs and alternate routes we did not anticipate on the journey ahead. No matter what it looks like, we must continue to follow our life map and listen to our inner voice that says, "Take the road to success, never give up, make a U-turn, in 2.5 miles continue praying, failure up ahead, keep watch of life's speed bumps that might try to slow you down." Even while in traffic, you must ask God for patience no matter how long you must sit in it.

I have not yet made it to my destination and have had many "pit stops" along the way. In 2006, I met the love of my life; in 2009, I was crowned Miss Morris College and in 2010, I graduated cum laude from the illustrious Morris College. In 2012, I opened the K. Lynese Center for the Arts, and in 2014 my handsome, healthy baby boy was born. In 2015, my K. Lynese team won their very first dance competition out of 44 teams from all over the United States and in 2016, the love of my life made me his fiancé. In 2017, I survived sepsis and married the man of my dreams. In 2018, this is where my life slowed down.

The signs I alluded to earlier were ahead of me. I sacrificed my dream and took an unplanned, yet necessary U-turn. My sweet and supportive mother became ill, and being the oldest of my siblings, I immediately acted and became her caregiver. It was time to be there for the woman who was my first coach and the one who has always been there for me. My role as my mother's caregiver led to me close my dance studio and quit a career that I always wanted as a news producer.

From February 18, 2018, to November 6, 2018, I reflected on the words my mother told me after losing the Miss Timberland Pageant.

"What's next Shakara? You are a natural born leader and a queen; do not give up!"

Now, the roles were reversed, and I asked her, "What's next, Mommy? I need you. Keep fighting, and do not give up." My mom fought pulmonary fibrosis for six years and her last words to me were, "Shakara, you are a strong woman. You got this!" Those words are stamped in my personal life's billboard; anytime I feel like my road is coming to an end, I replay my mom's last words.

After closing the K. Lynese Center for The Arts in January 2019, I renamed it K. Lynese Dance Company LLC and opened three locations. In February 2019, I was given the opportunity to become the new national director and choreographer for National Miss

UNCF Coronation. To date, in the months of April and May, I have coached four pageant contestants and won all four titles. In June 2019, my husband and I became homeowners. In October of 2019, I became a fulltime cosmetology student, which happens to be another passion of mine. In 2020, the world practically stopped due to the coronavirus pandemic. Some may think Shakara is crazy for thinking this, but I was thankful for yet another pitstop in my life. During this time, God knows I was about to go full speed in my life's journey because there is so much I want to accomplish.

Let us go back to February 20, 2020. That day was filled with joy and tears when my husband and I found out we were expecting. We had just suffered a miscarriage prior to finding out we were expecting. I honestly did not know how to feel, but then I thought, *why not me*? So many questions and yet, I was not paying attention to the big picture. Who would have thought after the world took a pause, my body was able to as well? Then, there it was—a tremendous blessing from God!

We were pregnant seventeen days after the miscarriage. After every storm, there is truly a rainbow. I couldn't wait to meet my miracle baby. On March 29, 2020, I tossed and turned. I could not sleep knowing I was beginning online classes the next morning. Who would have thought my mother would come visit me in my dreams?

"Sit down, Shakara and Asa. I'm about to have your gender reveal!" My mom said in my dream. I replied, "No, mom. We loss the baby, was no longer pregnant." She gave me that *oh you do not know what our God can do look*. She stressed to me in the dream that I was pregnant, and had revealed that it was a girl, but it was twins. When I woke up, I felt so nauseous and instantly called my husband to tell him we were pregnant. He said, "Well Shakara, let us get a test." Later that evening, my life took a shift. I was so elated that my doctor told us that this was a very promising pregnancy, and the baby had an extraordinarily strong heartbeat.

On November 21, 2020, we gave birth to our handsome baby boy, better known as Gov. Tyler Jaxson Parks. At twenty-one weeks, my husband and I were very concerned about giving birth in a hospital due to COVID. We then decided to go the all-natural route and do a water birth at a birthing center. Some had their opinions, but nonetheless, as a strong black queen I knew physically and mentally I could do it, and it was a great experience.

Today, I am Shakara Parks, author, choreographer, owner of the K. Lynese Dance Company, LLC and host of "The Nu-Experience Radio Show." After life's challenges, I thought my dreams and aspirations were completely diminished. In March 2021, I was granted the opportunity to join the WDRBMEDIA family. My weekly 30-minute program airs on Thursdays at 9:00 p.m. EST bringing Nu Flava, Nu Visions, Nu Attitudes and a Nu Awakening with a dedicated weekly segment focus on small business owners and talents around the nation.

This pandemic has molded me into someone who will enjoy the little things and family times. I believe in miracles, have discovered new passion, embraces every possibility, keep my faith and trust in God. I show gratitude, follow my heart in decision making because my life is now! I look forward to sharing my story and networking with other queens.

Remember these words: "The measure of a true queen is how many queens you have molded into the women they are today."

About Shakara L. Parks

Shakara L. Parks is a proud native of Pineville SC; she is the mother of two handsome boys Ayden J. Parks and the wife of Asa Parks III. Shakara is one of four children of O'Toole and the Late Linnea Smalls Theirse. She attended the public schools of Berkeley County graduating from Timberland High School in 2006. She furthered her education at Morris College in Sumter, SC and was crowned Miss Morris College 2009-2010 receiving her Bachelors in Fine Arts in 2010 with Cum Laude honors. Shakara is known internationally for her triple threat abilities in dancing/choreography, singing and acting.

Because of her well-known talents and dedication, she began her career at the age of 14 as a choreographer. Today she choreographs routines for many organizations, pageants, churches, coronations, weddings, and music artist around the South Atlantic Region and Internationally. Shakara also serves her community through her sorority, Alpha Kappa Alpha Sorority INC. in which she became part of the Nu Gamma Chapter of Morris College in the Fall of 2007. February 2018 Shakara became the Director and Choreographer for the National Miss UNCF Coronation. Shakara is the host of her very own radio broadcast "The Nu-Experience Radio Show" with WDRBmedia on IHeart Radio. She is also an author in the first anthology "The HBCU Experience Queens Edition.

February 2017, Shakara was diagnosed with Sepsis, which is the body's overactive response to an infection in the body. More than 1 million Americans are diagnosed with this infection each year and estimated that between 28% and 50% of those diagnosed do not make it. After surviving Shakara made it her duty to bring awareness which saved a lot of lives. She stands strong with other survivors but she didn't allow Sepsis to hold her back. Shakara is now bringing awareness to the lungs disease Pulmonary Fibrosis her mother battled for 6 years.

Shakara is passionate about serving her community, mentoring young women and putting a smile on each and everyone's face that she encounters. She believes that we can all make change in this world only if we all play our part.

CANDACE MICHELE JOHNSON

Remy Ma

Candace Michele Johnson

Miss North Carolina A&T State University 2007-2008

A quote from female rapper Remy Ma's, hit song "I'm Conceited" solidified one of the best decisions I've ever made as a young adult.

See this ain't nuttin' that you use to, out of the ordinary and usual. You gotta have the mind of state like I'm so great, can't nobody do it like you do.

And to be clear, I'm the furthest from the song title (my mother raised me better than that); but in all seriousness, that song led me to a path I will always be grateful for.

During the fall of 2004, my parents released my hand as I began my journey into young adulthood as a freshman at North Carolina A&T (NCA&T). During that time, some would have described me as an overly animated/dramatic, pigeon-toed, goofy, free spirited country gal with a big smile from South Carolina. Coming from a small town and entering into a pretty nice-sized university was a bit intimidating. I didn't know my place or even how to fit in. This feeling was foreign to me because I never cared about being accepted. I've always danced to the beat of my own drum. However, coming from a rural area and being exposed to new, beautiful people such as my peers with that "DC/Maryland swag," New York/New Jersey appeal, and the Cali coolness, was brand new to me. My university could be described as a "melting pot of black folk," but for some reason, I felt I did belong in that pot.

So, of course, when you're young, naïve, and somewhat sheltered, you try to do any and everything to fit in. Without telling all of my secrets, I probably experimented with something just to say that I was a part of something. But little did I know the party/roller coaster ride was just getting started.

Every day, I attempt to listen and follow the path God has for me, even if I don't agree with Him at times. However, one thing I'm sure of is that He gave me the spiritual gift of service.

I recognized I possessed that gift at an early age. This is largely due to my parents instilling the importance of being of service to others—within reason, especially if given the opportunity to do so. With that being said, I found my way during second semester of my freshman year when I decided to join the Senate. The Senate is a branch of the Student Government Association. I've always had the desire to be the voice of my peers, especially if I'm very passionate about something that will lead to positive outcomes. Serving in the Senate gave me that opportunity. I was finally finding my place and my purpose within the big blue sea of North Carolina A&T.

During my time within the Senate, I encountered a beautiful person inside and out named Ms. Anisah Rasheed. One of the most authentic souls I've ever encountered, I vividly remember Anisah wearing a gorgeous hijab and fly a** sneakers. She took interest in not only my background, but in my wants and needs as a new student. This was very rare to meet a human being as such.

About two months after my initial encounter with her, campus campaign season began. I caught buzz that she was running for Miss A&T for the 2005-2006 school year. And to be completely transparent, I've always held the assumption that a campus queen was strictly about pageantry, glitz and glamour, perfection, and the inability to be their true self. I'm aware that is a loaded assumption, but I didn't have true knowledge behind the role. Anisah's authenticity made such an impact on me, I was compelled to do my own independent research on what the position of campus queen truly embodied. I discovered the role was the furthest thing away from a pageant queen; a campus queen is a *service queen*. And then the lightbulb came on.

As expected, Anisah became the reigning Miss NCA&T 2005-2006, which was during my first semester of my sophomore year. I was blessed enough to assist her with her reign, which consisted of coordinating different community service projects and being the listening ear to our peers. Assisting her allowed me to dig deeper regarding one of my purposes in life, which is service. Occasionally, a small voice would jump into my head and whisper, "Candace, knock at the idea of Miss A&T, and not for your benefit but for the benefit of the community." I literally felt like Mike Tyson, fighting at that thought because someone like myself who was a non-polished, sneaker wearing party starter was not a typical campus queen, but the homie. God said He had something up His sleeve.

Time flies when you don't allow yourself to live in the moment. When I finally slowed down, I looked up and noticed that Anisha's reign had ended, and it was my junior year. In all honesty, junior year was literally the best yet worst years of my college experience. At that time, I was battling with who I was as a person and almost had a sense of hopelessness for unknown reasons. It truly felt as if a dark cloud had taken over my spirit. No one would've even noticed because to the naked eye, I was the "without a care in the world" Candace. But I thank God for a praying mother, because it's almost as if her prayers caused me to have a mental shift overnight, which was a great thing. However, that tugging thought regarding the idea of running for Miss A&T came back even heavier than before.

It was difficult for me to listen to God's direction because I had the constant mental battle of believing my peers wouldn't take me seriously to represent them and our community, as I didn't fit the textbook. I wasn't the description. But as previously mentioned, Remy Ma was about to play a huge role in my decision.

I was having a conversation with a close friend regarding the decision to run for Miss NCA&T or not. I could sense that I was irritating her due to me feeling sorry for myself and exhibiting a lack of confidence. During the conversation, she basically told me if I wanted to speak to her, I needed to learn and rap the first verse of "I'm Conceited" before any conversation we had. Once I heard her request, I thought I was being "Punk'd" by Ashton Kutcher, but she was serious. Her reasoning behind the task was for me to truly understand the essence of the song, and to live and breathe the words. The song's title can be misleading, however it's about a woman owning *who* she is, staying authentic to herself, and following her path. That moment sparked my final decision to hopefully become Miss North Carolina Agricultural and Technical State University 2007-2008.

Well, let's just say the ride was not easy. I was in my second semester of my junior year. I majored in nursing—a beast in itself, while attempting to campaign, be present and display to my peers because I wanted them to trust me to represent them. And a quick secret—I was almost disqualified. To be considered for the position, I had to participate in a showcase where each contestant displayed their oratory skills, talents and most importantly, to voice what our platforms for the community and campus would consist of. On the day of, I almost overslept and missed the entire showcase due to sleep deprivation. I had way too much on my plate at the time. It took some of my closest friends, who I'm still close with to this day, to bang down my apartment door and wake me out of a deep slumber to participate. However, after that real life nightmare, God saw fit, and my peers trusted me and voted for me to represent them for the 2007-2008 school year.

Although I wasn't the most polished, I knew I had a strong calling on my life to serve others and my peers recognized that. As a result, I was granted the position. Becoming Miss A&T gave me the resources and ability to place heavy focus on serving, not only my school community but the surrounding areas as well. I can truly say that saved me emotionally and mentally, and for that, I am forever grateful. I'm the woman I am today due to the universe working in my favor and teaching me the true meaning of selflessness while growing into a lioness.

About Candace Michele Johnson

Candace Michele Johnson (CMJ) has roots that stem from the southeast and northeast regions of the United States. However, she was primarily raised in Columbia by way of Manning and Charleston, SC. She is the daughter of Carl and Rosetta Johnson and the sister to Mrs. Carla Johnson Taylor. She is also the aunt to two beautiful nieces.

Candace graduated from North Carolina Agricultural and Technical State University Spring 2008 where she obtained a Bachelor's of Art in Psychology and was blessed with the unforgettable experience serving as Miss North Carolina A&T State University 2007-2008 during her senior year. She also possesses a Masters of Science in Clinical Psychology.

Professionally, she is a licensed board certified mental health therapist and received her clinical training from Dekalb Medical Center located in Decatur, GA. Currently she is in private practice within Alpharetta, GA and specializes in Major Depression and Anxiety amongst the young adult population.

Outside of her professional work, Candace is an aspiring TV screenwriter and Entrepreneur with a passion for all things nostalgic. She is also well versed in all things pop culture and a 1990s enthusiast. Over the recent years she discovered that one of her main passions is being able to reach the masses in positive ways via the arts and storytelling. She also places a high value on her religion, family, and values genuine friendship. Her lifelong motto is to "always utilize each set of 24 hours God gives you, because once they are gone, you can't get them back".

AHVERY N. THOMAS, ESQ.

Mirrored Inspiration

Ahvery N. Thomas, Esq.

Miss Grambling State University 2009-2010

As the Royal Court at Grambling State University, we were used as an extension of the recruitment department. We visited high schools and middle schools often to encourage students and bring awareness to the existence of HBCUs. Even though in these spaces, I felt as if we, the Royal Court, we were making a change in youth's lives, it seemed as if something was missing. Ms. Junior, now my best friend, Marquetta and I started thinking that we should reach out to the elementary school level as well. Within the week, a local elementary school called and asked if the Royal Court would be available to host an etiquette day for the young ladies in the fifth-grade class. It was perfect timing; to me, it was God's plan. We set the date and the school advised us to wear pink for the program.

One December afternoon, we all showed up in our pink luncheon suits from Bayou Classic that was held the week before. Perfect, right? We were then welcomed by the principal and the assistant principal. They showed us around the school. Eventually, we were taken to the library where the program would be held. The library was decorated in pink and silver. The plates were set out for the snacks, and the books were stacked and ready for posture practice. The desks were placed in a circle to have open discussion, and mirrors were set up at each space for hair and make-up tutorial.

The young ladies came in, fresh from recess. We welcomed them as they came in. As you'd think most little girls would be, they were mesmerized by our suits, sashes, and crowns.

"Wooooow," many of the little girls exclaimed with bright eyes and mouths wide open. Totally enamored with our outfits, some even asked if they could touch our sashes and crowns.

"Of course, you can," we assured them with smiles. One by one, we introduced ourselves, then asked the girls to introduce themselves. However, I noticed one young lady in the back who did not react to us being there. In fact, you could tell by her disposition that she wanted no parts of the "Pretty in Pink" program. I asked her name.

"Kennedi," she stated under her breath. This concerned me, but then paid it no mind. I figured she'd be okay after a while.

We started with an ice breaker with a random question.

"What is your favorite song?" We asked the girls. Back then, I had an iPod with the speaker dock. So, if I had a song that they liked on my iPod, I played a snippet. One young lady stated that her favorite song was "Obsessed" by Mariah Carey. When I asked her why, she responded, "Because these haters obsessed."

"Excuse me, ma'am," I responded before playing a snippet. They all started singing to the top of their lungs. The next song that was blurted out was "Ice Cream Paint Job" by Dorrough. Once I pressed play, everyone started dancing. On beat, off beat—no matter how they moved, they were dancing. Next, I heard "Pretty Wings" by Maxwell.

"Why this song?" I asked, totally intrigued by the fact that a fifth grader loved this song. She was shy at first, but then she asked if she could come up and tell me because she did not want to say it out loud. I said, "Okay." She walked up to me, and I bent down to her level so she could whisper it to me. She told me that it reminded her of her mom who passed the year before. She said that she believes her mom has pretty wings right now. I looked at her and my shoulders dropped. Looking into her eyes, I gave her a big hug and told her, "I am sure your mother has beautiful wings." I played a snippet of the song just for her.

The last song was "Swag Surf" by Fast Life Yungstaz. Now, we all know what this song can do. Every person got up and started dancing—not necessarily doing the dance associated with the song, but doing something close to it or as close as fifth graders could get to the dance. At this point, I noticed Kennedi was still not amused by our program. How do you not get up for Swag Surf? It is still a classic to this day.

Next on the agenda: make-up and hair. Now, since they were in fifth grade, we decided not do too much. We had some washable makeup kits that we got from the dollar store for them to play in. They had blush, eyeshadow, and lip gloss. We also had combs and brushes if they'd like help to fix or tidy up their hair. We made sure to ask if their moms would be okay with it. Some were truthful and said their mom would not allow it.

"That's okay; you guys can help us help your classmates," we assured them. While working on hair and make-up, we also talked about hygiene and the best practices for caring for ourselves. We brought facial wipes to help them take off the makeup and how to properly remove makeup. We also allowed questions about different types of body soaps, deodorants, and body types. We discussed types of clothing, how to put outfits together and how to accessorize. Kennedi still did not include herself in the activities.

Our next activity was eating etiquette and posture. We did the walking posture first before sitting down to eat. I waved at Kennedi and asked, "Do you want to join?"

"No."

"Well, would you like any snacks?"

"Yes."

"No posture practice, no snacks," I told her. Kennedi got up to do the posture practice, but by the look on her face, you could tell she would rather not participate. She got up slowly, dragged her feet as she got in line with the other girls. I handed her a book to place on her head. She rolled her eyes and dropped her head back as she took the book from my hand.

All of the girls now had books on their heads. Their shoulders were back, and they walked around the library, making sure not to drop the books. For Kennedi, her book kept falling. After her book fell again, some of the girls started laughing at her. She threw the book down and stormed off as if she was about the leave. One of the school employees went after her and told her that she would lose her privileges to be at "Pretty in Pink." I went over to see if I could help.

"What's wrong?" I asked Kennedi.

"Nothing," she responded with an attitude.

"It does not seem to be nothing."

With her arms crossed, she did not respond. I reminded her that we had snacks and I would like for her to stay and eat with us. I asked her if she would stay. She nodded her head yes. I told her that I needed to hear her say "yes."

"Yes," she responded. I grabbed her hand and took her over to get some food. Before I started to eat, the school employee asked for a word with me. She brought me outside the library and explained to me that Kennedi had been having some issues at home. As a result, she started acting out in school and her grades are now suffering. I told her that I would try to talk to her.

I went and sat beside Kennedi while we were eating our snacks. I asked her how she was feeling. She shrugged her shoulders. I asked how the snacks tasted.

"Good," Kennedi responded.

"How is school?" She shrugged again. I told her that I heard that she has great grades.

"Not anymore."

"Why?" I asked.

"I don't know."

"You are very smart and very beautiful, and you should show the world how smart and beautiful you are." That's when she smiled. I then complimented her on her clothes. She leaned over to me and whispered, "I don't really like pink."

"Me either," I whispered back to her. We laughed.

Our last activity was teaching the girls the meaning of an *affirmation*. After explaining what an affirmation is, Ms. Junior and I gave examples. Their last job of the program was to stand up and speak life into themselves with their affirmation, starting with "I am." Kennedi was the last one to go.

"I am beautiful, and I am smart," Kennedi affirmed. We smiled at each other as we and the others clapped. The girls got back in line to go back to class. I asked the school employee if I could speak with Kennedi for a second, and she allowed it. I told Kennedi that I was proud of her and happy that she decided to participate. She nodded her head and got back in line to leave the library.

As the day went on, I thought about Kennedi and what type of future she would have. I hoped that I helped. I hoped that I made her feel good about herself and encouraged her. I hoped that I was able to speak life into her.

After a couple of weeks, I went to my office on campus and saw a pink envelope in the file holder on my door. I opened envelope as I walked in. I put my purse down on the desk and sat in my chair to read it. The envelope said: "To: Miss Grambling State University,

From: Kennedi." Inside was a pink "Thank You" card from her.

"Thank you for everything you did for me. I am happy that you came to my school. P.S. I am doing better in all of my classes."

As my eyes watered, I sat back and thought to myself that she actually has inspired me. From that moment, that letter from Kennedi showed me that you never know whose life you can inspire or change in a positive way. Because of this, I wanted to be a better person. My intentions that day were to inspire fifth graders—speak into them, encourage them. I did not realize that I would be the one who would be inspired by them. You never know who is watching you and who can be inspired by you, or *who can inspire you.*

About Ahvery N. Thomas, Esq.

Ahvery Thomas is from the small collegiate town of Grambling, La. Here, she graduated from the laboratory school. She then enrolled and graduated from the HBCU located in the same town, Grambling State University. Here is where she was elected, Miss Grambling State University, 2009-2010. She pledged the Delta Iota Chapter of Delta Sigma Theta. She graduated with a Bachelor of Science degree in Business Management and a Master of Science in Sports Administration. She then worked for a Fortune 500 company, J. P. Morgan Chase, for a year. She left that job when she was accepted into law school at Southern University Law Center. She then began to work in the Athletics Department on campus and at the Sun Belt Conference in New Orleans, La. After graduating from Law School and passing the Louisiana Bar Exam, she was promoted to the Director of NCAA Compliance and Title IX Investigator. She later started serving her community by taking a job at the Legal Services firm working with foster children. She is now a practicing attorney in the Baton Rouge area.

I'm her free time, she enjoys volunteering with helping feed those who are less fortunate and mentoring the youth. She also enjoys reading, writing, and spending time with family and friends.

Her aspirations in life is to own her own law firm and become a successful entrepreneur owning businesses that not only add to the economy within the community but give second chances to youth. She also wants to start a non-profit focusing on those youth in need the second chances.

Ahvery Thomas is the daughter of educators, Dr. Edwin B Thomas, Sr. and Rhonda Thomas. She has two siblings, Ahsaki Thomas and Edwin B. Thomas, Jr. She is also an Auntie to her lovely niece, Zharia Thomas.

JADA CRISP

90 Stories to Tell
Jada Crisp
Miss Tennessee State University 2019-2020

Serving as the 90th Miss Tennessee State University was truly one of the most distinct honors of my life. As a little girl, I never dreamed of becoming a queen. I didn't think it was in my plans; nevertheless, the crowns found me. Although I was basketball homecoming queen and Miss Bolton High School, becoming a HBCU queen was life changing. This massive role serves as a change agent and force in our HBCU community. It gave me my greatest gifts, memories, and lifelong friends. I strived to be the queen of my university to showcase an ordinary girl serving and wanting to make a change.

Inspiration to Lead

My freshman year, I spotted the reigning queen the night of her coronation. As a first-year student, you sometimes perceive a top four student position on campus as a little out of your depth. She was gorgeous and very down to earth, I thought, *if she could run, I could too*. That night, I prayed and asked God that if Miss Tennessee State was in His will for me, to lead the way. Before I knew it, He did just that! I simultaneously gained everything I needed in preparation of becoming queen.

After I've had time to process it all and reminisce on my reign, I look back on my life and realize that God ordered my steps. Early on in my collegiate career, I joined numerous organizations that developed my growth over the years. My junior year, I decided that I was going to campaign for Miss TSU. What a nervous time in my life! I had been preparing and crying months before the election had even started. I persevered and conquered every battle I encountered. I was hungry for the position and could not wait to serve the university in that capacity.

I remember the day like it was yesterday! On Friday, April 5, 2019, at 3 p.m., as we gathered in the amphitheater, it was announced that I won. My body instantly felt a rush; I cried, prayed, and jumped for joy! After receiving the title, I immediately went to work. There was a mother and young daughter on campus. The mother approached me and informed me that her daughter was having difficulties at school. She asked if I would speak with her, and of course, I didn't turn down a chance to feed our future with knowledge. Later in the year, I was able to see her again during the Homecoming Parade! To this day, her mom continues to inform me that she has progressed since our little discussion. By far my favorite assignments were those that involved the youth.

The Standard

The female student body mentor, sister, and friend. The blueprint of every young lady on campus. Miss Tennessee State University is traditional, transformative and forever timeless. Of course, the position of queen had its intense moments, but we often forget that it's not about the "glitter and glam." It's about serving the greater good. Being Miss TSU is a political role of good meaning and service, it's also not only about that either. It's about the *impact* you make on your campus, and how it effects the students, faculty, and staff. I wholeheartedly hated to impress someone; that was not my place. My role was to inspire, enhance and embrace our tiger pride on all levels. With an open-door policy, I was always a listening ear and a solution operator. My job was to put every young woman on a pedestal and help them identify themselves as a queen. My Miss TSU advisor would be watching from a distance and say, "You're like a magnet; people literally connect with you."

I'd walk around campus just to speak and hang out with students. I wanted them to know that I'm a natural girl who does the same exact things they do. A few goals of mine were to truly enhance campus culture, to attract and retain all students. To overcome number two, you had to complete number one first. If it doesn't give you joy to spend quality time with the student body, this role may not be a good choice for you. You must love your institution, love what it stands for and be willing to go to battle for it in rooms. It cannot defend itself.

I naturally care for people, so transitioning into a public servant role wasn't hard. However, it gets intense when you're tired; but you still must perform. My personal motto on the royal court was "Stay ready so you don't have to get ready." As a queen, you have many appearances to make—from community service, high teas, conferences, to all student-related events on and off campus.

You had to have "the look." It took me roughly two hours to prepare for an event. As you can imagine, I participated in numerous public speaking engagements; therefore, I had to be quick on my feet. Whatever the university or my advisor asked of me, they knew I'd provide. People would think I was just sitting there smiling, but I was memorizing my script in my head or reading the audience to know what level I needed to perform to. Preparing myself for any question or task, I wanted to give my all on every occasion. I worked hard to leave my mark and create an everlasting legacy.

The Golden Court

My experience serving on the royal court was a monumental season for my life. I was blessed to come in with humble, hardworking individuals. We started out as strangers, but we ended as The Golden Court. Our mission as a court was to genuinely be bonded with our student body and upkeep our university's motto. We were given the opportunity to be a voice for so many lives and so many students. We diluted the stigma of needing to be popular or serving a previous royal role. Our goal was to make every peer know that their voice was needed, and that each student made a difference. Every impression wasn't extravagant; but as long as it was effective. I always prayed to God that when people see, hear and feel us, that they see Him, hear Him and feel Him for His glory.

I was hard on my court about our representation. I wanted us to show up and demonstrate excellence always. When you're a queen, you must make the smartest decisions for the entire court, even if they're hard judgments. As a leader, it's hard not to overstep into an advisory role, but I had to realize that I'm a student, too. Our amazing advisor Tasha Andrews didn't play, she supported us!

Sometimes, I wish I could revisit memories, live in the moment, and enjoy every second serving with my court. Although there is no perfect court, we had joyful and delicate moments. But nonetheless, I wouldn't have been able to complete my reign without them. We complemented each other very well, and I'm not talking about looks. We built a *family*. Although Covid-19 compressed the end of our reign, we didn't let it make our reign. We had a beautiful time, and an amazing reign! I'd be remiss if I did not mention the bond that we still have even to this day. Countless group messages and FaceTime conversations hold our connection steady.

Lead with Love

We were always presented well, but only if people knew what it takes to have an out-the-door, ready-to-go smile. The position taught me about mental health and how to take care of me. As a student leader, you're often pulled from different directions of the university. You must be recharged by doing whatever gives you happiness to keep going. Concurrently, you must look good mentally, emotionally, and spiritually to pour into others.

You must remember that you're always your position. People will always associate you with your position, even *after* your reign. If you're "on E," how can you fill someone else up?

Each student had a different struggle to face every day, and I believe I eased as much as I could by being a breath of fresh air on campus. I was someone the student body knew they could confide in. Any chance I get to speak with current students, I say, "Cherish college." There will never be another time that you'll be together in one community with unlimited resources. Of course, they'll be rough patches with relationships and adjustments. However, don't let anyone box you in. You'll grow through people in this role, just as you would in any transformative moment. Be creative, be you and serve with integrity.

Being an HBCU queen gave me more than fancy material; it gave me wonderful acquaintances, kings and queens from all over. I gained more than I expected, I was blessed to pour into so many people's lives and for so many blessed people to pour into me.

To all my queens reading this chapter, your life is your reign; cherish your reign, set your boundaries, and do what it takes to achieve.

About Jada Crisp

Jada Janyce Crisp was born in Memphis, TN March 12th 1998. She was born to her parents James Chaney, Ira Crisp Sr., and Rhonda Garland. She is the middle sibling of Ira, Naudia, and Iraianna Crisp. Jada studied Business Administration with a concentration in Supply Chain Management. She continues her journey with TSU, by writing her signature on the world and being an active alumna in the DFW Alumni Chapter. With a strong work ethic, she has correspondingly managed several extracurricular activities aside from her academics including, Executive Planning Leader of Supply Chain Management Student Organization, Alpha Kappa Psi Professional Business Fraternity Incorporated, Delta Sigma Theta Sorority Incorporated and the University's Honors program, for she served as a proud member. In addition, Jada has interned at two Supply Chain Governing Board Partners, including HCA and The Boeing Company. When she isn't giving time to her respective organizations or business endeavors, Jada enjoys trying new coffee shops, traveling, and hanging out with her friends. After graduation, Jada relocated to Dallas-Fort Worth, Texas to pursue her plans of Aeronautics Sustainment. Although her plate seems full, she keeps God first and values her education as she gives back to the community and uplift everyone she encounters. During Jada's reign as Miss Tennessee State University, she strived to be a great representation of the young women at TSU while remaining transparent, loving, relatable and genuine.

OLIVIA TURNER

Taking a Chance
Olivia Turner
Miss Texas Southern University 2012-2013

It never occurred to me until my junior year of high school that I wanted to go to college out of state. I had a list of California universities I wanted to attend and was ready to be a "Cali girl" forever. The beginning of my HBCU journey started when I ran for Black Student Union President for Perris High School and for second vice president of United Black Student Unions of California (UBSUC). Both were extracurricular positions that would look great on my college application, but soon would turn into the most inspiring experience that would impact my life in ways I couldn't have imagined. It was from this moment, I would host the first Black College Fair at my high school, attend state and regional conferences and gain a true understanding of how deep the black college culture went.

As I was preparing to select a college to attend, I knew I wouldn't be able to visit all the out-of-state colleges on my list. I received scholarships from a few, so it helped narrow down my choices to those offering financial support, because let's face it, tuition isn't cheap. Of all these places, I knew two things: one, I would not get a chance to visit campus before accepting; and two, I would not have any family in the area. Once I set my mind to the idea of something, I have to make that vision come true. So, I decided—with a bit of hesitation, that I would pick an out-of-state university I had never visited. My first steps on Texas Southern University's campus would also be my first steps on HBCU soil.

My parents packed down my car, hitched it to the back of my dad's truck and we drove from California to Texas. When they drove off, I started to question my decision. I've always had my parents watching over me. I have always had my little brother by my side.

"This experience will make or break me," I thought to myself. I am here to tell you my collegiate experience was all that I needed it to be because I am proud of who I am today.

Freshman year set the pace for the rest of my college experience. I made friends, I attended Labor Day Classic, Battle of the Bands, joined different organizations and worked for the athletics department. Juggling school and work, and simple things like having lunch in the "caf" with my classmates, kept things funny and alive. I remember seeing Miss Texas Southern University for the first time at a football game, walking the track and waving. "I want to be just like her," I thought. She was so classy and elegant. Her presence from afar was inspiring enough.

At age 20, I was crowned Miss Texas Southern University. This was an accomplishment that I knew I had to invest in completely. I remember the feeling I had when I first introduced myself as "The Queen," and the first time I had my crown placed on my head. *Extraordinary.* A young girl from Perris, California had made her way to Houston, Texas and made her dreams come true. With holding such a high honor, I knew that I had the opportunity to expand my platform for education reform at my university and for the community.

Creating a platform helped me confirm what I am passionate about. I loved math, but I loved people more. My platform's mission was "Bridging the gap between mathematics and minorities." Math is a universal language we all need to know, whether it is calculating the grade you need on a final to pass a class or trying to recall the logic behind theories.

Senior year was the bittersweet end to a journey that started 1,500 miles away. The moment I worked so hard for. The successes and failures, the internships and jobs, the laughs and the cries. All I could think was, *"I did it!"* I walked across the stage with a Bachelor of

Science in Mathematics, and I felt ready for the next chapter in my life. I attended the Thurgood Marshall College Fund Leadership Institute the prior year and had secured a position as a cyber security analyst at a consulting firm. Just a few weeks after graduation, my career began.

The village carried me across that stage. The people who believed in me—my family and friends, carried me across that stage. A mental reel of my journey played back in my head, and there were no regrets; however, there were a few gems that I would keep in my heart.

1. **Believe in yourself.** Is it easier said than done? The idea isn't perfection. The idea is giving yourself enough grace for growth. Every day, we actively choose to decide on how we feel about ourselves. During worry, self-doubt, and failure, we understand that this was a part of the journey, but it does not define who we are.

2. **HBCU is family.** When you attend a black college or university, you will walk away with aunties, uncles, sisters, brothers, cousins, etc. You will meet people from all walks of life, and you will make friends that will last a lifetime. There will be people who care about your entire existence and will love you for *who* you are. Homecoming will be the best family reunion every year.

3. **Just Do It.** There were many times I've felt fear behind making decisions. Set the intention and give it your all. The journey won't be easy, but it will be worth it. You are only one decision away from being a step closer to who you choose to be.

4. **Spread the word.** Not everyone has access to someone who has had a HBCU experience. As a proud graduate, I will let you know that black colleges and universities need to be on your list and strongly considered. My collegiate experience at Texas Southern University is irreplaceable and I will always advocate for students to experience it.

I would like to thank my mother and father, Theresa Turner and Elliott Turner, for their abundant support and respect for my decisions and opinions. I want to thank my little brother, Elliott I. Turner, for always reminding me that your craft is gold and not to take everything so serious. To my friends who have been there through the ups and downs, I thank you from the bottom of my heart for keeping me balanced. Thank you Mrs. Mellany Patrong and Mrs. Paula Kimble for supporting my endeavors. To my son, Isaiah, you are my world and I love you so much.

About Olivia Turner

Olivia Turner is a native Californian who pursued her dream of attending an HBCU. Ms. Turner, without a campus visit, decided that Texas Southern University would be her home after graduating from Perris High School. Ms. Turner graduated with a Bachelors of Science in Mathematics and a minor in Health Studies.

During her tenure at Texas Southern University, she played an integral role in several impactful organizations on campus such as Society of Urban Mathematicians, Habitat for Humanity, National Organization of Black Chemists and Chemical Engineers, Tiger Yearbook, Collegiate 100 Black Women and the National Society for Black Engineers. She is a member of the Delta Gamma chapter of Delta Sigma Theta Incorporated.

With a focus on high academic achievement and volunteerism, Ms. Turner was a recipient of TSU's Louis Stokes Alliance Minority Participation Scholarship, the Thomas F. Freeman Honors Scholarship, the Marine Corps Scholarship Foundation Scholarship, Scholarships for Military Children and Wooten Grant recipient. Miss Turner served as a Marine Corps Scholarship Ambassador, TSU COST Student Ambassador, Black Student Union Ambassador, and a U.S. Dream Academy Mentor.

Miss Turner served as Miss Texas Southern University 2012. During her reign, she focused heavily on education reform. Her platform, "Bridging the gap between mathematics and minorities," was created in order to close the educational gap between students and mathematics by providing skills and development through mentorship. Ms. Turner won 2nd Place in the Verizon Ultimate Reign competition and used the prize winnings to host the first TSU Tiger Games, which was a high school mathematics competition for

Houston inner city schools. She also funded two scholarships for undergraduate students with STEM focused degrees.

After graduating Cum Laude, Miss Turner went on to pursue a career in cyber security and information technology. With the knowledge and experience gained throughout her professional career, she volunteers with STEM programs and participates on panels to give insight on how to jumpstart your career in consulting and technology. Currently, Olivia is a Senior Cyber Engineer for Deloitte, a multinational professional services network with offices in over 150 countries and territories around the world.

In her spare time, Ms. Turner enjoys spending time with her son, running, traveling and celebrating life with family and friends. In the future, Olivia hopes to be remembered as someone who was a role model for individuals from underrepresented communities and willing to open the door for others so their path to greatness can be fulfilled.

AIRNECIA MILLS

The Dream, The Test, The Victory
Airnecia Mills
Miss Alcorn State University 2012-2013

Dreams really do come true.

I come from a family of "Alcornites". My aunties, Vanessa Mills-Wigfall, Youlanda Mills-Walker, Debra Mills, my stepfather, Lamar Swint, and my cousin Jacqueline Bruce-Tubbs all graduated from Alcorn State University. Currently, my cousin, Oniyah Robinson attends ASU. I went from attending the games and admiring the cheerleaders and the royal court, to cheering on the field and representing my school as Miss Alcorn State University, 2012-2013.

It was December 2011, and I was sitting in my bed talking to my roommate, who's also a fellow cheerleader.

"Carmen, I think I want to run for Miss Alcorn."

"Really, Air? I think you would be a great queen."

"Yes, I would love to represent the university and serve."

I immediately texted my mom, Althea Robinson-Swint, my sister, Markeisha Robinson, and my grandparents, Oliver and Margie Robinson, to share my interest in running for Miss Alcorn. My family was very supportive and loved the idea. They were so happy!

I wasn't sure if I would be able to run for the position because although I was classified as a junior, I had only been at the university for two years. I came in as a freshman but had over twelve credit hours from my dual enrollment courses in high school. This allowed me to enroll as a sophomore my first year at Alcorn. I worked hard during my senior year of high school and took all of my prerequisite classes. Because of my drive and hard work throughout grade school, I was determined to graduate college in three years.

As I matriculated through college, I was very much involved on campus. I was a student ambassador, member of Student National Education Association (SNEA), and a cheerleader. Along with being a recipient of various awards and accolades, I accomplished my goal of graduating from college in three years with a Bachelor of Science in Elementary Education with a minor in Special Education and Reading. Two years later, I graduated with my master's from Alcorn in Elementary Education.

After campaigning, putting up many signs, posters, giving out treats, and barbequing, participating in the Miss ASU pageant and competing in a runoff, I was crowned as Miss Alcorn State University in 2012. I was so overjoyed by the love and support shown by my Alcorn family. My coronation was definitely "A Cinderella Story."

"Air, are you really crying?" I was asked. Yes, I cried during my entire speech. I was so grateful that God allowed this to happen for me. The Lord gave me this opportunity and I was so overjoyed. My student body believed in me. To walk in the gym and see the beautiful set up made me feel like Cinderella herself. My family traveled from all over to support me. Former queen, sorority sister and mentor Mrs. Shequeta Wells-Murphy, was my mistress of ceremony, and many former queens were in attendance and showed much love.

During my reign as Miss ASU, I implemented many initiatives on campus. One of my very first initiatives was "Get fit with the Queen," an initiative that allowed young ladies and young men on campus to come together to work out and get fit. I also implemented a "Queen's Tea" for the young ladies on campus. The Queen's Tea united young ladies on campus together to be encouraged by former queens. I was so grateful for the former queens who came back to campus to speak and motivate the young ladies at my tea. I was blessed with the opportunity to travel, attend many conferences and trainings such as the Queen's Connection and NASAP Student Leadership Institute. I loved the speaking engagements. I enjoyed speaking to students, future Alcornites, and Alcornites all over the world.

Another highlight of my reign was being featured in *Ebony* Magazine during my reign. That feature was definitely one to remember; in fact, it was *amazing*! Ten HBCU Queens were selected by votes to be featured in the magazine. We traveled to Atlanta, Georgia to shoot for the magazine with celebrity photographer Derek Blanks. We experienced a day of pampering and a full makeover. While in Atlanta, we met several celebrities, bonded, formed relationships and shared our many experiences.

Many great things happened for me during my reign. I was initiated into Alpha Kappa Alpha Sorority, Incorporated. I was also afforded the opportunity to do my student teaching to prepare for graduation. I passed all of my required assessments for my educator's license (Praxis 1, Praxis 2 and the PLT). Before I could move into my core courses for my degree, I had to pass praxis 1 and 2. I did not pass Praxis 1 on the first try and I became so discouraged because I felt as though I was under pressure, but I studied hard and paced myself just in time to move into the next phase of my program. Graduating in three years was my dream, but I didn't realize the pressure that came with it. Next up was the last exam, the PLT (Principles of Learning) assessment. To apply for graduation, I had to have this test passed by a certain deadline. Well, the Friday right before Thanksgiving beak I took the PLT. I studied hard, prayed, and waited patiently on my results. Imagine waiting on your results over the Thanksgiving break and sitting at Thanksgiving dinner thinking about a test. Guess what? Three weeks later my results were in, and I passed my test. My three years of undergrad were over. Also, during my reign, I was blessed to be able to walk the field as Miss Alcorn and cheer during basketball season. I loved to cheer, and cheering was my heart. So, I was extremely grateful for the opportunity to do both.

Being an HBCU Queen molded me into the person I am today. As a result, I am even more driven and passionate about serving people. In my current role as an assistant principal, I serve the community, educators, and children. Education is truly my passion. I love children, and I love to see them grow. I also love to help other people grow. I live by the motto Dr. Martin Luther King quoted from a song: *If I can help somebody as I pass along, if I can cheer somebody with a word or song, if I can show somebody he's traveling wrong, then my living will not be in vain.*

Being an HBCU Queen has taught me courage. It has taught me to take a leap of faith and to always keep pushing. After college, my goal was to go back home to give back to my community. I wanted to make a big impact while serving the community. After teaching first grade for two years, I realized that my community needed an after school tutoring center. In 2015, I opened my very own tutoring center. My tutoring center has helped students from kindergarten through college with test prep, homework assistance, and tutoring. During the pandemic, I was able to get my very first book vending machine. Because I wanted to find a way to keep children reading and engaged, I created a book vending machine and placed it in Oak Court Mall in Memphis, Tennessee. The vending machine has books, bookmarks, and reading lights inside. It has been very successful. During the pandemic, I partnered with my cousin, Marchetta Parker, and we are co-owners of a trucking company, M & P New Heights, LLC.

After completing my Specialist Degree in Educational Leadership from Arkansas State University in 2020, I was determined to continue to "climb the ladder". Prior to completing my specialist in Educational Leadership, I passed my SLLA (School Leaders Licensure Assessment) in 2019. I was very inspired to become a principal, but I also wanted to relocate. Well, Atlanta has always been my dream. After college I wanted to relocate to Atlanta, but I wanted to go home, Greenville, MS, to give back to my community first. Nine years later, I was finally ready to flap my wings and become a resident of Atlanta.

I put in my application for my licensure and set out to explore job opportunities in leadership. I did not sign my contract to return to my current position because I was stepping out on faith, and I was positive that I as supposed to be in Atlanta. Six months had passed, and I was struggling with finding a leadership position. I had contacted every district in the city, was flying back and forth for interviews and school visits and everything started to become very frustrating and stressful. Finally, I received an offer from an academy in Atlanta for an Instructional Coach position. Well, the same day of the offer, I was informed that there was an Assistant Principal position open in my current district and the opportunity was there. I was so overwhelmed with emotions, yet so undecided. I had waited for six months for a position and the same day that I finally got a position, I was offered an Assistant Principal position. I prayed about the opportunity and talked it over with my family. God definitely had big plans for me. Maybe Atlanta was not where He wanted me to be, or maybe not yet. I accepted the Assistant Principal position because it was the better opportunity, and it was exactly what I wanted. It may have not been in the city that I wanted it to be in, but it was right where it needed to be. I realized that sometimes what we want is not exactly what God wants for us or maybe He has something bigger and better in store. I am so happy that I waited patiently on God, and He blessed me with the opportunity to become an Assistant Principal. I am looking forward what God has in store for me.

One of my favorite things about being an HBCU queen was networking and meeting people all over the world. It has taught me the importance of relationships and networking. I was afforded the opportunity to build relationships with so many mentors such as motivational speaker Keith Brown, who still supports me and reminds me that anything is *possible*. I've built relationships that will last forever. I am thankful for my Alcorn family. We continually encourage and motivate each other to be our best. We are our own support system; we support and congratulate each other on each other's accomplishments.

I am so grateful for the opportunity to become the queen of my HBCU, Alcorn State University. I am thankful for my peers who believed in me; for my advisor, Ms. Hogan, who encouraged me and continues to support me today. I am grateful for my former cheer coach, Ms. Brown, my AKA advisor, Dr. Smith, who supported me throughout my entire reign, and my roommate, cheer mate, and campaign manager, Carmen Campbell- Lewis.

I want to continually be a role model for young ladies all around the world. I want them to know that no matter what they are faced with, they can do it. With God on their side, they can do anything that they put in their hearts to do. My next goal is to become Dr. Mills. I am currently completing my doctoral degree at Belhaven University. This has been a very interesting journey, late nights, early mornings, migraines, counselors and tutors, but I am so glad that I didn't give up and I decided to continue to pursue my doctoral degree. In December 2021, I'll be "All but dissertation". My plan is to complete my dissertation in one year and graduate as Dr. Mills by December 2022. This is truly my dream and has always been my goal. I am so thankful for the process because God does everything for a reason. My favorite Scriptures are *I can do all things through Christ which strengthens me* (Philippians 4:13) and *For I know the plans I have for you says the Lord...* (Jeremiah 29:11). I am still on my journey to success and my goal is to help someone along the way.

About Airnecia Mills

*"She is clothed with strength and dignity, and she laughs
without fear of the future." –*Proverbs 31:25

Determined, motivated, and outgoing, I am Airnecia Mills, a native of Greenville, MS. I received my Bachelors in 2013 and Masters Degree in 2015 from Alcorn State University in Elementary Education with Reading and Special Education endorsements. While undergrad at Alcorn, I pledged Alpha Kappa Alpha Sorority, Inc., was a student ambassador, and was Miss Alcorn State University. I graduated from Arkansas State University in 2020 with my Specialist Degree in Educational Leadership. My dream and biggest goal is to become Dr. Mills. Currently, I am enrolled in the Doctorate of Education in Educational Leadership program at Belhaven University.

Upon completing my bachelor's degree, I moved back home to teach and give back to my community. My first teaching job was in Greenville Public School District as a first grade teacher. After three years, I transferred to Hollandale School District in Hollandale, MS. While in Hollandale School District, I served as a SPED Case Manager, SPED Inclusion teacher, 11th Grade ELA teacher, and cheer coach. Three years later, I was blessed with an opportunity to become an Academic Coach in Sunflower County Consolidated School District. Currently, I serve as the Assistant Principal of Lockard Elementary School in Sunflower County. I am grateful for my many blessings and opportunities to grow as I continue to impact the lives of others.

I am the owner and founder of Mills Academy, an after-school tutoring center in my hometown, Greenville, MS. At the academy, we focus on tutoring students Pre-K to 12th Grade. We specialize in homework assistance, test prep, and tutorial. Mills Academy was established in 2016 in efforts to give back to my community. I also wanted to help struggling learners and provide enrichment services for gifted students.

In 2020, during the pandemic, I became the owner of Mills Academy's Book Vending Machine. The book vending machine is located in the Oak Court Mall in Memphis, TN. It contains books for students in all grades and of all ages.

I attend Rose Hill North Baptist Church in Greenville, MS, where I serve in the choir. My grandfather, Rev. Oliver Robinson, Sr. is my Pastor. My favorite scripture is Jeremiah 29:11, *"For I know the plans I have for you," declares the Lord, "plans to prosper you and not harm you, plans to give you a hope and a future."*

In my spare time, I find great pleasure in reading and researching, tutoring, helping others, and mentoring young girls. I enjoy traveling and exploring new states and countries.

TAYLOR BELLE

Grace To Lead

Taylor Belle

Miss Wilberforce University 2017-2018

Wilberforce University, the nation's first private HBCU, was founded in 1856 in Wilberforce, Ohio. Named after abolitionist William Wilberforce, Wilberforce is rich in history with distinguished alumni such as Bayard Rustin, Leontyne Price, and Dorothy Vaughn. As a stop on the Underground Railroad, walking on the grounds of Wilberforce feels like I'm following my ancestor's steps. With the notoriety of Wilberforce, I was intimidated to even pursue the position of Miss Wilberforce University.

As a Dayton, Ohio native, I did not hear much about HBCUs. I attended a small high school in west Dayton, with a total student count of about 300-400 students. I was an exceptional student, graduating as valedictorian of my class with a 4.2 GPA. Due to my scholastic achievements, prestigious predominantly white institutions were recommended to satiate my desire for knowledge. I received a full ride to another university and attended for two years. When I stepped foot on Wilberforce's campus, I immediately fell in love with the culture. The welcome that I felt from the faculty, staff and the students was astounding. They didn't know me, but it was like they knew no strangers. Anybody who stepped foot on that campus were treated as family. At that moment, I knew that I had to transfer.

I spent a year getting acclimated to the campus, picking up extra curriculars like being a tour guide, an ambassador, and doing community service any chance I could. I maintained a 3.6 grade point average because I knew what position my heart desired. Walking down the hallway of the King building, I finally seen a Miss Wilberforce University informational flyer. I was scared, I was nervous, but I was also excited. I tried to do everything in secrecy so that I could back out if I got too scared. In my mind, who did I think I was, trying to be a queen of Wilberforce after just being there for one year? What makes me think that I am qualified enough to get selected for a position such as this? I tried to ensure that I did not look at who my competition would be, because that would add another layer of anxiety for me.

I shared my aspirations with a select few of my friends, and some of the faculty who I held close to me. I had a close friend of mine put me through "Queen Bootcamp." We worked together tirelessly to ensure that I would be ready for the pageant. For the first time since I had this idea, I felt ready.

The pageant went by quickly. Due to the bootcamp that I went through, it almost felt like a breeze. The moment I was waiting for finally came: Who would be Mister and Miss Wilberforce University? We only had one male vying for Mister Wilberforce, so we understood that he would be our next king. I and two other girls just put on an amazing show for the audience and were waiting for the results.

"Your 2017-2018 Miss Wilberforce University is…"

At that moment, everything went quiet. I felt my heart beating out of my chest. I could not see anyone in the crowd; it felt like it was just the three of us. I closed my eyes so that I would not tremble in front of everyone watching us.

"Taylor Belle!"

I couldn't believe it. I could not believe that I won. All the late nights and the worries came to pay off. I hugged the two other girls on the stage and stayed to take pictures. It felt unreal.

The one thing I learned during my bootcamp, was that the moment after you've won, everything changes. I was no longer just "Taylor the transfer." What I wore, what my hair looked like, what my grades were, even my outside activities were a topic of discussion. Although

I've always done well in anything I've ever done, I've never been directly in the spotlight in that way. I've never been shy and was always an outgoing person, but I became a walking billboard. I worked during the summer to ensure that when I went back to school, I could be the best queen that I could be.

I was preparing for the HBCU Kings and Queens Conference in July of that year. It was in New Orleans, a place that I have never been but always wanted to go. I would be around royal courts of schools across the country. These schools are bigger than mine and they are familiar with each other. How could I represent my small university to the best of my ability? How could I show everyone what Wilberforce had to offer? My advisor at the time drove us thirteen hours to New Orleans because she seen how badly we wanted to go. I couldn't believe that she agreed to it, but I'll be forever indebted to her for it. The Kings and Queens Conference was one of the best experiences of my reign. I learned things, I networked with other kings and queens, and my Miss Senior even won an award. Although I was nervous about my reign, I knew that this was just the place I needed to be.

I started the school year ready and refreshed. I had so many ideas and so many different things that I wanted to be a part of and do. During my reign, I was a lead resident assistant and cheerleader at Wilberforce. I wanted to make sure that people seen me everywhere and understood that I was a different type of queen. The goal I set for myself at the Kings and Queens Conference was that I wanted to be multifaceted. I wanted my peers to see me handle queen business, be a president's list student, a student athlete and still have my fun as well. My king and I assisted with anything that we could on campus as a way to ensure we were still student connected. We assisted in weekly meetings for homecoming while planning our coronation. It was nerve wracking and frustrating, but yet it was an amazing experience. We received gifts and love from our peers that we didn't expect, and truly felt the love that people had for us.

I had my doubts and worries about my reign. Coming from a smaller HBCU, you do not have the same opportunities as larger HBCUs for exposure and participation. They had opportunities to speak at major events both nationally and locally. They have opportunities to speak about themselves and their universities in such high regard that it would leave people curious about who they are and who they represented. I was discouraged with competitions that required votes and outside participation. I was a girl from a small town in Ohio from one of the two HBCUs in Ohio. Where did I think that I could compete with some of these larger, publicly funded schools? I wanted to ensure that not only I represented my university to the best of my abilities, but myself as well.

I had a heart to heart with a previous Miss Wilberforce from 2014-2015. She helped me grasp the idea that it is not always the position, but the person in it. Regardless of if you're aware of it or not, you're influencing someone, and you're making a mark in your own way.

When I thought about it, I did more during my reign than I ever thought I could. I was able to be a speaker on a panel for UNCF during their tour in Cincinnati, an opportunity that I did not believe that I would have. I would be a part of HBCU Campaign's Campus Queen spread, I was able to attend the mayor's luncheons, be a part of various photoshoots, and have my picture listed in *Ebony* Magazine. It is easy to get caught in the glitz and the glamour of what a queen is. It is easy to compare yourself to others in a position such as this, and it is very easy to be unkind to yourself during a reign. My experiences at Miss Wilberforce have made a much stronger woman out of me. I went through many personal struggles during this reign, but queendom has taught me how to lead with my best foot forward, regardless of what is happening around me. I've learned how to handle things with grace and poise, while staying true to myself and my overall goals.

I am grateful to Wilberforce for allowing me the amazing opportunity of representing such a university with an extensive history. I learned so much about myself during this reign. I learned how to be a better leader, and how to make the best out of the opportunities that I have, regardless of what I have seen others with. I truly hope that my reign was an experience that someone else could learn from and look up to.

About Taylor Belle

Taylor Belle is a native of Dayton, Ohio. A 2020 graduate of Wilberforce University, the nation's First private HBCU, Taylor served in a plethora of leadership roles including President of Delta Sigma Theta Sorority, Inc. Beta Chapter, and SGA President. Most notably, Taylor served as the 2017-2018 Miss Wilberforce University. Taylor served with the platform of "Encouraging leadHERship: Honesty, Empowerment, Resilience." Taylor's primary focus was to change the culture of a leader through servant leadership and motivate the campus population to be multifaceted achievers. Currently, Taylor works with children and families in social work and is continuing her education to obtain her master's degree. Taylor enjoys giving back to her community by organizing acts of community service in her area. Taylor lives by the quote "Solid women don't crumble" and hopes to continue to motivate young men and women to reach their goals and full potential.

BETH INABINETT

Echoes of a Golden Era
Reflections and Memories of My Reign as the Fiftieth Miss South Carolina State College

Beth Inabinett

Miss South Carolina State University 1987-1988

Friday, September 18, 1987, I was crowned the 50th Miss South Carolina State College (SCSC) by the second Miss South Carolina State—the oldest living queen at the time, Mrs. Gracia Waterman Dawson (1936 – 1937). I was the second Miss SCSC from my hometown of Frogmore Community on Saint Helena Island, SC to Betty Jean Richardson Brown (1959 – 1960). I was the successor of my cousin, Janet Abigail Williams Simmons. Janet was a newly commissioned officer, so she was unable to make the journey overseas for my coronation.

My coronation's theme was "Echoes of a Golden Era." It was a golden era indeed, filled with valuable experiences, life lessons, meeting and greeting people—young and old from all walks of life, travel, dear friends and cherished memories.

When I agreed to be a part of this wonderful publication, I was not prepared for the surge of beautiful memories that mixed with old fears and insecurities. Honestly, back then, I didn't see myself as the pageant girl. I didn't feel comfortable or confident enough to enter and compete with far more beautiful, intelligent and talented young ladies. Plus, I was a stutterer like my father, although, much to my surprise, my stutter never occurred while singing. I absolutely feared the Q & A segment because I didn't want to be ridiculed or embarrassed. We can thank and blame my bossy Alpha Phi Alpha Fraternity, Inc.; friends for strongly encouraging me to compete in their Miss Black & Gold pageant

"You're going to run!" They all said. Well, I competed; and much to my surprise, *I won*!

This journey actually began Thursday, September 18, 1986, exactly one year before my coronation. We were all in the gym rehearsing the dance routine to Chaka Khan's *Eye to Eye* for my Cousin Janet's coronation. I represented Miss Black and Gold, and my escort was my great friend, Keith Williams. Keith had such a radiant smile, a heart of gold and a spirit to match. In between our rehearsal, we stood around, admiring the beautiful setting. The stage, lights, decorations—everything was perfect. Then the sweet soul looked me square in my eyes and said,

"You're going to be the next Miss State College."

"Boy, please! Not me!" I exclaimed in my classic "geechie girl" style. Although I was laughing, he looked serious, and repeated his prophecy. He went on to tell me why he believed it would be. "You're pretty, you're popular; you're nice, you're cool, you're funny; people like you, and you can sing." I humbly thanked him, but quickly dismissed the silly idea that the student body would elect me to represent them. I didn't entertain the thought for another six months. His brothers approached me in the cafeteria and pretty much told me, "You're going to run." My initial thought was, 'well, I survived competing for a vocalist slot on the jazz band my freshman year; competed my sophomore year for a slot on the Champagne Dancers squad; and won Miss Alpha Phi Alpha the end of my sophomore year, so I should be ok competing for Miss State College."

Did I believe I could win? Not a chance, or so I made myself to believe, especially with all of the other excuses I'd mentioned earlier. I was not affiliated with a sorority at the time, so I just knew I would not have a chance. I called my parents after I signed up to run and they both wished me luck. My mother reminded me to "just be you." My father reminded me give it my all. The Most High God *always* kept me covered. He placed me in the midst of great genuine souls—

family, friends, faculty, staff who all breathed and spoke life into me, set me straight when I was out of order, and supported me throughout the campaign and my reign.

Everything changed in February of 1988. My friend, Keith, died unexpectedly on campus. This left me with too many questions, sleepless nights, sadness, depression and grief. I missed an entire month of class because I didn't quite know how to handle what I was experiencing. I went to work at *Camelot Music* in attempt to escape my reality. Music was always a source of healing for me, so working there was indeed medicine for my soul. To top matters, I knew at that point I was not a candidate for the May 1988 graduation, which really made me feel like I'd let my family and the university down.

I called my father in tears that March, thinking he would be compassionate and sympathetic. Boy, was I wrong! He saw my grades and went off. The conversation was one of tough love, and a colorful array of cuss words. He reminded me that I still had work to do, and a major mission to accomplish—to graduate. Dad told me that I'd better go get some help. He suffered from PTSD as a result of childhood and adult/military trauma. He knew the importance of having a healthy state of mind. That phone call quickly sent me on campus to begin the hard, yet long overdue, necessary conversations with my professors and health professionals to get me back on track.

Everything I experienced that year greatly impacted my life forever. My journey gave me the confidence and courage to pursue my dreams passionately and unapologetically; to take countless leaps of faith, step out of comfort zones, face reality and conquer my fears. It inspired me to help myself and others heal, to conquer infertility and become a mother at ages 36 ½ and 41 and pursue my passion for singing and helping others. The experience was the groundwork I needed in order to present and perform before diverse audiences, ranging from classrooms and congregations, to performing on stage with a band and alongside a few of my favorite artists. In addition, it set me in motion to relocate to Dayton, Ohio from 1990-1997. I enrolled in The University of Dayton's graduate studies program in September 1991, where I studied counseling and psychology. I graduated with a 4.0 grade point average on August 4, 1993. I've worked in the counseling profession for nearly thirty years.

In July 2020, I started my business, BeTHeLiGhT, LLC, "a Sole to Soul, Root to Crown Soulful Service provider for seekers of love, peace and SOULutions for a greater and purposeful life." It's a play on words of my first name, and a charge for us to empower, encourage, uplift, support, hold space, model, teach, promote healing, self-love, and love for God and humanity. It is where my passion for God, love, life, music and healing intersects.

It's been nearly thirty-four years since coronation, and the indescribable range of feelings from fear to joy, excitement and gratitude from those moments in time still touch my heart. I've managed to hold on to my yearbook, a few precious pictures, a VHS recording of my coronation, my coronation program, and other campaign and pageant memorabilia to help me relive those special moments. I humbly rejoice and give thanks for the purposeful journey and the once in a lifetime experience of representing not only the university and the student body, but my family and hometown as well. It is an honor to be a part of a great legacy, and I will cherish it all forever.

About Beth Inabinett

Beth Maureen Inabinett is a proud Gullah Geechie native and current resident of Saint Helena Island, Beaufort County, South Carolina. She hailed as the 50th Miss South Carolina State College from 1987 – 1988.

Beth is the mother of two sons, Zuhri (2002) and Solomon (2007,) and a fur-baby named Amber (2012.)

Beth is the lead singer/songwriter/vocal arranger of *The Inabinett Project*, a South Carolina based band composed of an impressive group of musicians who are committed to providing the best musical experience with every show. They are known for their crowd-pleasing performances and vast repertoire of music that encompasses a wide spectrum of genres spanning jazz, rhythm & blues, pop, funk, classic rock & reggae. Beth is also a vocalist with the Columbia, SC based band – *The SoulJazz Collective*, and the Beaufort, SC based band, *The RK's*. Beth has been singing professionally since the age of 15, and has shared the stage with several notable artists, to include Meli'sa Morgan, Angela Bofill, Frank McComb, Bobby Wilson, son of the late Jackie Wilson, the late Kofi Burbridge (Tedeschi Trucks Band,) Carl Thomas, fellow SC State Jazz Band vocalist and former member of the R&B group *Blackstreet* Mark Middleton, Saxophonists Jeannette Harris and Dee Lucas, Trumpeter and fellow SC State University alum Willie Bradley, The Spinners, and fellow Saint Helena Island native and American Season 12 Winner Candice Glover. In 2010, Beth nearly lost her ability to sing when during a medical procedure, her vocal cords were bruised. Fortunately, the surgery to repair the damage was successful. Nevertheless, fear kept the songbird from singing for nearly 5 years. Thankfully, she overcame that obstacle through prayer, meditation, family support, and voice therapy.

In addition, Beth is an Ordained Minister, Reiki Master, Certified Labor and Postpartum Doula, Placenta Encapsulation Specialist, SC Notary Public, and a licensed hair braider. She is the creator and owner of *BE*THeLiGhT, LLC*, a holistic health and wellness and spiritual empowerment source, whose mission is to serve as a root to crown soulful service provider for seekers and believers of love, peace, knowledge and solutions for a greater and more purposeful life journey.

Beth has nearly 30 years of counseling and education career experience to include college, academic and career counseling, vocational training and rehabilitation, mental health/psychiatric services, health care, adoptions/foster care, and community-related services. She has held certification in the area of Guidance - Secondary in the state of South Carolina, and Guidance PK-12 in the state of Georgia.

Beth was initiated into the Nu Delta Omega Chapter of Alpha Kappa Alpha Sorority, Incorporated, in Beaufort, SC on August 22, 1999.

Beth was inducted into the SC State University Jazz Band Hall of Fame in 2019, along with 12 other recipients including Fred Wesley, Willie Bradley, David Haynes, and the late Angela Clark.

Beth was born May 5, 1966 to the late Heyward Inabinett of Islandton, SC, and Shirley Brown Inabinett of Frogmore, SC. She is the younger sister to Sharon and Gail, and the older sister to Heyward (Reggie) II. Beth's father was a diesel mechanic and private pilot, eventually teaching his 2 youngest children how to fly. Her mother retired after 48 years as Owner/Operator of Shirley's Hairstyling Boutique. Beth's passion for music and song began at the age of three and continues today. She credits her mother, whom she hails as her favorite singer, her late Aunt Evelyn Brown Burke, and her sisters Sharon and Gail for inspiring and influencing her love for music. She credits her late father as her biggest fan.

During her teens, Beth was actively involved with the local Civil Air Patrol unit, where her father was the Unit Commander. She received a flight scholarship through the organization, and earned a Solo Pilot License at the age of 16, thus becoming one of the youngest and first black females to receive a license. She became a licensed School Bus Driver one month later. Beth was promoted to the rank of cadet Lieutenant Colonel prior to graduating from Beaufort High School in 1984.

Beth is as 1989 graduate of South Carolina State College, where she received a Bachelor of Science in General Home Economics, with concentrations in Child Development/Early Childhood Education, and Elementary Education. During her years at SC State, Beth was a vocalist in the SC State College Jazz Band, a Champagne Dancer on the Marching 101, and sang 2nd Alto on the concert choir. She was crowned Miss Alpha Phi Alpha Fraternity, Inc., during her junior year. Beth earned a Master of Science in Education from the University of Dayton in August 1993, completing her studies with a 4.0 GPA.

RACHEL D. INABINETT

My Experience at Morris College
The Real Choice
Rachel D. Inabinett
Miss Morris College 1988-1989

It was Friday, the fourteenth of October, nineteen hundred and eighty-eight at eight o'clock in the evening, when I was officially recognized and crowned Miss Morris College,1988-89. That was so long ago, but it reigns supreme as one of the most memorable experiences in my life.

I entered Morris College in August 1985 to learn, and I departed in May 1989 to serve. As a graduate of one of the many Historic Black Colleges and Universities (HBCU), I believe that black colleges and universities are the root of the black community. The first HBCUs were founded before the American Civil War to educate black youths who were intentionally denied a quality education. For over one hundred and fifty years, the primary available means for educating blacks at collegiate level was the Historic Black College.

Many black colleges were founded as state colleges to teach former slaves the significance of being educated black men and women. The roots of HBCUs must be traced to the significant black leaders during the post-Civil War period who fought to ensure that all black children would be educated. Black leaders, who were not intimidated by the fact that segregated schools overlooked black students by providing quality education to white students. These black leaders realized that our problems were not self-inflicted. Therefore, they took it upon themselves to act, to initiate, to promote, to regulate, to provide, to encourage, to attain and to introduce to black youth our primary alternative for education: *The black college indeed*!

HBCUs are facing challenges to continue providing higher educational opportunities for blacks and continue striving for excellence. HBCUs are among the most prominent educational institutions in our nation. Morris College and other HBCUs provided strength, pride, leadership, respect, academic achievement, high aspirations, saw to the needs of the black community and knowledge of the black heritage; but above all, HBCUs uplift black willpower to learn, to live and deal with society with the utmost respect and professionalism.

HBCUs educate us about *us*. We learn our history. At HBCUs, we learn that former illiterate slave blacksmith, James W. C. Pennington learned to read and write in English, Greek, Latin, and German, and also wrote the first major history of black people. We also learn that Dr. John Rock coined the term, "Black is Beautiful."

After attending a predominately white high school, attending Morris College was a wonderful, pleasant experience. Every day, I saw people who looked like me, and that in itself, was a reward. I gained so many new friends who really cared about me. I was excited to grow, to learn and to prepare for success. Going to college can be frightening to some individuals, but I felt welcomed at Morris College. I had new friends and a new life. As a graduate of Morris College, I have gained a lifetime of rewards that I will treasure forever.

My freshman year, I attended the Miss Morris College Coronation. Dressed in a pink cocktail dress, I arrived early so that I could get a good seat. I had no idea what to expect. I attended pageants before, but never a coronation. It was nothing like the high school pageant I competed in; this was different, but in a special way. I was so moved by this event that I made up my mind—that night, to be Miss Morris College. At the end of my junior year, I competed for Miss Morris College and won. I was so happy. It was an awesome experience representing Morris College.

Morris College has afforded me so much. Most of all, attending Morris prepared me for graduate school and so much more. I learned to really think and use my brain power. I challenged myself to be great just like the people who looked like me. Once I started maximizing my brain power, I was a new individual. I believed I could conquer the world. My experience at Morris College did that for me. I will always be grateful to Morris College.

I would like to share words of wisdom from Dr. Dennis Kimbro, author of *Think and Grow Rich: A Black Choice*, who talked about one of the least respected parts of the body—the human mind. He stated that the human mind is the last great unexplored continent on earth. It contains riches – material and spiritual – beyond our wildest dreams. Like any fertile field, the mind will return anything planted. Our minds come to us as standard equipment at birth, it is free. Predictably, we place little or no value on that which is given to us for nothing. On the other hand, things that we pay for, we value. Everything that is really worthwhile in life comes to us free. Our minds, our souls, our bodies, our hopes, our dreams, our ambitions, our intelligence, our love of family and true friends, these priceless possessions are free. This is in line with my Morris College education.

I agree with the well-known hip-hop artist, the late Heavy D, when he said, "I believe in being believed in." My experience at Morris College presented an opportunity to me every day, to know that someone—other than myself, knew my capacity for greatness. I will never forget the impact Morris has played in my life.

On any given day, when I visit the campus, I am reminded of greatness. Greatness, because I had the privilege and honor to attend Morris College. Greatness, because of my family's legacy and history with Morris. When I visit the campus, I see Daniels Hall, named in honor of my grandfather, the late Dr. George Goings Daniels. I see the Anna D. Reuben,

Mamie Coker, Magnolia Lewis, Albertha Simons Hall (AMMA Hall), named in honor of these great women, including my aunt, the late Dr. Anna D. Reuben. I am reminded of being on campus as a little girl, when my father, the late Dr. Rufus J. Daniels served on the trustee board and attended numerous events.

I have a heart filled with cheer, because of Morris College. All hail to thee!

About Rachel Daniels Inabinett

Rachel Daniels Inabinett is from Conway, South Carolina. She reflects a varied personality including ambition and the qualities of thoughtfulness. She is a determined and vigorous individual, yet pleasantly calm. Rachel is motivated by learning new things and sharing knowledge. She is an avid reader who considers reading her greatest strength. She believes reading allows her to master anything.

She began her federal career in 1992 with the Department of Defense (DoD). She is a detailed-oriented and highly motivated Equal Employment Specialist with over 28 years of experience in employment law. She has held numerous positions with several DoD agencies. Her specialized experience includes serving as primary advisor to commanders, providing guidance/assistant to supervisors and employees on equal employment opportunity laws, rules, regulations, policies, programs, including special emphasis programs, complaints processing, affirmative employment and training. She currently serves as the Deputy Director/Complaints Manager, Equal Opportunity and Diversity Management Office, with a focus on compliance and strategic programs.

Rachel earned a B.A. in Political Science History/Pre-Law, Morris College and a M.A. in Human Resources Development, Webster University. In keeping with the Morris College motto "Enter to Learn, Depart to Serve," she continues to share her skills, knowledge and abilities in service to others.

APPOINTMENTS & SERVICE (Past and Present)
- Chair, Katie Floyd Daniels Scholarship Committee

- Chair, Strategic Planning Committee, Morris College National Alumni Association

- Chair, Homecoming Committee, Morris College National Alumni Association

- Life Member, Alpha Kappa Alpha Sorority, Incorporated

- Member, Morris College National Alumni Association

- Member, Budget Committee, Morris College National Alumni Association

- Member, Membership Committee, Morris College National Alumni Association

- Member, Program/Alumni Committee, Morris College National Alumni Association

- Member, Fundraising Committee, Morris College National Alumni Association

- Chair, HBCU for Life, Rho Chi Omega Chapter, Alpha Kappa Alpha Sorority, Incorporated

- Board of Directors – Leavenworth Community Service Organizations, Incorporated

- Treasurer – Upsilon Rho Omega Chapter, Alpha Kappa Alpha Sorority, Incorporated

- Treasurer – Leavenworth Community Service Organizations, Incorporated

- Public Relations Director – Leavenworth Community Service Organizations, Incorporated

- Morris College National Alumni Association Leadership Team

- Chief Financial Officer – First Missionary Baptist Church

- Parliamentarian – Upsilon Rho Omega Chapter, Alpha Kappa Alpha Sorority, Incorporated

- President, Upsilon Rho Omega Chapter, Alpha Kappa Alpha Sorority, Incorporated

- Mid-Western Region, Alpha Kappa Alpha, Nominating Committee

- Mid-Western Region, Alpha Kappa Alpha Conference Vendor Chairperson

- Secretary - Upsilon Rho Omega Chapter, Alpha Kappa Alpha Sorority, Incorporated

MARISA MANNING BRAXTON

The Journey to Becoming
Miss South Carolina State University

Marisa Manning Braxton

Miss South Carolina State University 1989-1990

"I can do all things through Christ who strengthens me."
–Philippians 4:13

Reflecting on my life's journey, the words of this Scripture have given me much comfort. But, if I'm truly honest, at the time I chose this Scripture as part of my reign as Miss South Carolina State University, there was still much doubt in my mind about my abilities and worth.

You see, I grew up the youngest of three in a small town in Georgia. My parents were well-known in the community; therefore, my siblings and I were exposed to a lot of opportunities. I grew up participating in all types of activities, and in many areas, I often found myself being the only African American. During my formative years, my hometown—though not legally segregated, still had not fully embraced the integration of races. With this in mind, when I found myself involved in opportunities as the only "one," I automatically assumed it was due to my parents' connections. Although I've achieved many great things prior to college, I left home not fully knowing that my success was due to my actions.

Arriving at South Carolina State was the beginning of my journey to self-validation. I was at home on a campus where no one knew me and yet, everyone looked like me. I immediately settled in and made lifelong friends. I started to find value in myself and recognized the impact I had on others through simple acts of kindness. My confidence developed as I recognized I was succeeding in school academically and socially. And more importantly, I was succeeding outside my parents' world.

Fast forward to my junior year. For years, I had been enamored with the former Miss South Carolina State University queens. Each queen offered so much to the role. The queen reigning during my junior year was Beth Inabinett, and she was such an inspiration. She was talented, kind, beautiful and well-respected. When I saw her carrying out her duties as Miss South Carolina State University, I wondered if I could possibly carry that title with as much grace. As quickly as I wondered the possibility, I questioned myself once again, "Who am I to think I could be Miss South Carolina State University?" I knew I was no longer the insecure young lady who arrived on campus my freshman year, but was I strong enough to vie for the biggest title and honor one could seek?

First, I sought advice from my parents, who gave me encouragement; and my close friends who gave me confirmation that I could carry the torch. The missing piece was *me* and the confidence I needed to believe that I could obtain the title. I remember turning to my favorite Scripture, Philippians 4:13, that says, *"I can do all things through Christ who strengthens me."* I had to meditate on it and cling to those words more than ever as I started my journey. I knew the journey would not be easy. There were so many other beautiful, smart, and talented ladies seeking the same title, and I knew all of them were equally excited as I to wear the crown. I decided to trust God's words, and I held on to the belief that I could do anything I set out to do. With each campaign flyer, speech and appearance, I gained the strength God had promised me.

The night of the pageant brought both excitement and fear, but I had come too far to turn around. I was determined to be the best me I could be. No matter the outcome, I knew I was better for having taken the journey. I had prepared for the night, and many of my supporters were in the audience. It was up to me to go forth and present my best self. Unfortunately, the night wasn't perfect.

Every segment of the night had gone just as planned, except the talent portion. I had a terrible performance. I chose to play a piano piece, and due to nerves, I missed a key. In that very moment, my confidence dropped. It was near impossible to get back on melody with my selection. That was it. All the work I had put into my campaign came down to that moment, and I was devastated. I left the stage horrified and in tears. It would have been easy to allow the embarrassment of the moment to convince me to walk away, but God gave me the strength to hold my head high and walk back on stage to face the student body for the remaining portions of the night.

At the end of the night, though I was unhappy with my talent performance, I realized it was just one moment of the night. In the end, I had given my best, and I was at peace. I don't really remember my thoughts as I awaited the results from the student body vote, but I can say I was not certain of a win, but prayerful. When the announcement was made, I was immediately filled with joy. I would be joining a legacy of women who I admired for so many years. And yes, it registered with me that this accomplishment came *without* my parents' connections. This accomplishment was mine, and I was beyond blessed with the honor. My sense of self and the ability to accomplish difficult dreams were validated in that moment.

As the title of Miss South Carolina State University started to set in, I began to reflect on the journey I took to get to this point. My parents were so proud of me, and my friends and classmates, too. *But why me?* Remember the pageant, and the poor talent performance? How could my classmates have overlooked that flaw and still vote for me? As more and more people congratulated me over the passing days, it became clearer to me how the road to Miss South Carolina State University started, and I realized my journey started long before the two-hour pageant, and long before my junior year. It was the three years I had spent on campus, treating others with kindness and respect. It was the day-to-day interactions I had with others over the years that would resonate with my colleagues.

It was the way I carried myself each day that counted more than anything I could have displayed over the course of a two-hour pageant. The title of Miss South Carolina State University was a culmination of me growing into my sense of self.

I won the title of Miss South Carolina State University in 1989, and thirty-two years later, I am still influenced by the lessons learned before, during and after my reign. Today I am a teacher of twenty-six years, and I have been blessed with the opportunity to shape the minds of so many young boys and girls. I am a wife and mother, and each day I make decisions for my family, trusting God each step of the way. I walk with confidence and pride. I instilled in my daughter a love of self so her journey to self-validation can be shorter than mine. It gives me joy when I can help others simply by being kind. So often, people assume greatness comes from things that can be accumulated; but I know it comes from the day-to-day impact made on the lives of others.

I pray my story resonates with some young person who's questioning if they are enough. I would advise her to trust in God for the strength needed to face any challenge, and to live each day with love and kindness towards others. For the future Miss South Carolina State University or any other queen, remember the campaign is not one night. It is the day-to-day role you play. Treat people with respect; and when you stumble and miss a key, they will overlook the flaw and remember who you are and what you represent.

About Marisa Braxton

Marisa Braxton is a proud alumnus of one of South Carolina's greatest HBCUs, South Carolina State University, where she graduated with a B. A. in English, and a minor in Education in 1989. She reigned as Miss South Carolina State University during the 1988-1989 school year, and was initiated into the Beta Sigma chapter of Alpha Kappa Alpha, Sorority, Inc. in 1987. After graduating from South Carolina State, she continued her education at Illinois State University, receiving a M. A. in English.

Marisa has devoted her professional life to enriching the lives of teenagers in the field of education. She has been an English teacher for over 25 years, and currently teaches English in the International Baccalaureate Program at Campbell High School in Smyrna, Georgia. In addition to her work in the classroom, she sponsors numerous clubs, and works diligently to promote positive outlets for youth to feel valued, nurtured and supported.

Marisa currently lives in the metro Atlanta area with her husband, daughter, and two fur babies. She continues to employ the lessons she gained as Miss South Carolina State University in her daily decisions.

ARLETTE KIM REIVES

A Queen

Arlette Kim Reives

Miss Barber-Scotia College 1986-1987

One day after attending classes on the sacred grounds of Barber-Scotia College, I was walking across the yard and Dr. Mable P. McLean, who was the president, tapped on her window and motioned me to her office. As my mind raced at the motion of the president, I immediately thought I was in trouble. Dr. McLean possessed a quiet strength that was expressed profoundly through her speech. She stated that she had watched my leadership abilities. She noticed that I served the faculty, staff and classmates in a well dignified manner. She appointed me Miss Barber-Scotia College simply based on those observations.

My soul identified with the sacred grounds of Barber-Scotia College. The school had begun as Scotia Seminary and the spirit of the place felt as though my soul had found its resting place. My spirit was aligned with the history of the institution. The appointment as the campus queen ignited a desire in me to learn as much as I could about the institution that I had been called by God to represent. This institution intentionally threaded Christian commitment to the powerful force of education. The beautiful intertwining of faith and education is found in the way human nature expresses itself. The soul of a person grows through experiences. My HBCU experience at Barber-Scotia College fine tuned my leadership skills.

As Miss BSC, I had the task of representing the college at various occasions. Homecoming was a special time to show off the leadership to the Alumni. I enjoyed leading the meetings with the Alumni and challenging them to give back to the college for my SGA to take the opportunities to greater heights. One of the highlights for Homecoming was the early morning parade. This was a time when the community would join in the celebration and forge ties that would enable young people to experience Scotia and hopefully one day attend the College.

Barber-Scotia College, like other institutions of its kind and time, was born out of the pain and tumult of the Civil War. (Cozart, 1970) As I researched and studied the history of the college, this institution had the audacious courage to generate faith that would move mountains as its charge was to educate first generation freed slaves. The spiritual presence on these sacred grounds was felt like home because I was the first to attend college in my immediate family. This experience allowed me to feel nurtured by a loving group of well educated, spirit driven people who cared about the student's wholistic wellbeing.

Scotia was founded as Scotia Seminary as a mission granted by God to produce students who were not afraid of hard physical work, open minded, and spirit driven. While I walked those grounds, the very spirit could be lived. I often found myself taking care of my professors. It was an honor to drive Dr. Cordery around on Saturday mornings, while listening to her stories of how Scotia helped form her as a woman in a male dominated space in the Presbyterian church. The stories she shared inspired me as a leader and helped me gain a strength on the inside that would remind me that I could because she did. There were many Sunday evenings when Dr. Newsome and Dr. McLean would have students over to their homes to share tea and cake. These were times when I would become submerged in their stories and how their experiences at Scotia or other HBCUs helped them become the leaders they were.

College Work-Study was a means of making extra money on campus. My work-study was in the Athletic Department. Mr. John Black from Kannapolis was the Athletic Director at the time. He was a proud member of the Omega Psi Phi Fraternity. He was a very proud AGGIE also and we would sit in the gym together as he would share his experiences as a student at A&T. He would talk to me about

A&T's Homecomings and all the positive energy that happened during that time. Scotia was his blessed haven and he wanted to make sure I understood the importance of keeping Scotia alive.

There was Dr. Deborah J. Calloway who was my softball Coach at Scotia and the first Delta that I had the privilege of getting to know. She often shared her experiences of her love for the HBCU. On many occasions Dr. Calloway would encourage me to make sure I went straight to Graduate School. She would talk about the potential I had, and that education is a driving force for change in this society. She would remind me of the responsibility I had as Miss BSC to lead others in a moral and ethical way. The expectation that I was charged with from these two Professors would help me see the World as a place of constant improvement and I had the tools to make it a better place for the next generation as they demonstrated through their work.

Growing up in Randleman, NC, which is a small rural town, the worship experience was a part of my weekly ritual. I have always had a strong spiritual connection and the ability to experience Vespers, our weekly worship service on campus, was needed in order to feel centered. On most Sundays, I was able to ride back to my hometown with the pastor of my home church because he and his family lived in Concord, NC. This gave me an opportunity to discuss social issues on and off campus with Pastor Roseman and how the issues should be addressed.

Scotia allowed me to tap into my spiritual and educational abilities. I hold a Master of Divinity degree from Hood Theological Seminary in Salisbury, NC which is located north of Barber-Scotia College. I am a proud graduate of that institution because of its continuation of education and spirituality of what I experienced at BSC. For me there has always been a spiritual emphasis when purpose is declared because God has the final say for our lives and trajectory. Vespers shaped my spiritual formation at Scotia and Hood reminded me to always stay connected to Barber-Scotia and represent her well.

The professors were more than professors, they were guides. There was a community developed on Scotia's grounds that had a World vision for the students. While I was obtaining my Master of Divinity degree, I was able to volunteer as Chaplain at Barber-Scotia and become the National Alumni Association Chaplain.

I currently serve as a founding member of the Judy Rashid Leadership Center in South Africa and the founding Pastor of the Amazing Joy Worship Center based out of Raleigh, NC which serves a group of Clergy members in Gauteng, South Africa. Education is freedom.

My Mentor, my friend, my other Mother, Dr. Judy Rashid is an instrument of grace, who I now share my story with as we build an educational leadership center together in South Africa to continue the legacy of those from whence we have come. The spirit must drive the educational in order for there to be transformation.

About Arlette Kim Reives

Reverend Arlette Kim Reives is a Servant leader; she has searched the scriptures and found that many are called but few are chosen. Matthew 22:14

Rev. Kim served as volunteer Chaplain at Barber-Scotia College in Concord, NC, her alma mater, Chaplain of the National Alumni Association of Barber-Scotia College, served as supply Pastor for the Empire Circuit of the United Methodist Church in Randolph County and recently an Associate Minister at Berean Baptist Church, Raleigh NC.

A native of Randleman, North Carolina, she graduated from Randleman High School and is known in the area for her natural athletic ability especially on the basketball court. While attending RHS and serving as team captain, she was selected Most Improved 1980-1981, Most Outstanding Athlete 1982-1983, and voted Player of the Year of Randolph County in 1982. She was a four sport letterman all four years of her high school career; she set many records in Basketball and Track and Field.

In 1983, her athletic ability was rewarded with a full basketball scholarship to attend Barber-Scotia College in Concord, North Carolina. She was noted on the Dean's List Spring 1985-1986 and fall of 1986-1987 while being recognized for High Academic Achievements and placed in the Who's Who Among students in American Universities and Colleges in 1987. Rev. Kim graduated from Barber-Scotia in May of 1987 reigning with the title of **Miss Barber-Scotia College** and was featured in *Ebony* Magazine. She received her Bachelor's of Science degree, cum laude, in Secondary Education.

She was employed with the Guilford County School system for 25 years as an educator and taught third through sixth grades while also coaching girl's basketball, boy's volleyball and special assistant to the football team. She coached the Eastern Middle School Girls basketball team to Conference Champions in 2000-2001 and 2001-2002 and served as Head Coach for the women's basketball team at Randleman High School.

Later she was employed as the Curriculum Facilitator with the Middle College on the campus of NCA&TSU. During her tenure the program was named a Blue Ribbon School by the U.S. Department of Education and named a School of Excellence and Distinction. The school was further noted for 100% graduation and College Acceptance in 2012.

In 2013, she was inducted into the Hall of Fame at Randleman High School as the first African American Female to ever receive the award.

Rev. Reives was licensed in 1999 and ordained in 2003 under the Pastoral Care of the late Reverend Joseph Duke, Pastor Emeriti of Outreach Missionary Baptist, Inc. Greensboro, North Carolina. She received the Master's of Divinity degree from Hood Theological Seminary Salisbury, NC in May, 2013. She has served in ministry for 21 years and in 2019 became the Founding Pastor of the AMAZING JOY WOSHIP CENTER in Pretoria, South Africa.

As a Servant Leader, she ministers in the spirit of the motto of her Alma Mater: ***For, Head, Heart and Hand***. Her favorite scripture to date is Romans 8:31 *"... if God be for us, who can be against us?"*

Rev. Reives is also intrigued by the Last Will and Testament of her fellow alumnus, the great Mary McLeod Bethune: "I leave you Love, love builds. It is positive and helpful. It is more beneficial than hate."

DARCELE JONES-HORTON

From a College Girl to a College Queen
Darcele Jones-Horton
Miss South Carolina State University 1989-1990

Determined, diligent, and dedicated are just a few ways to describe how I live, love, and express myself. These attributes activated my belief that I could be Miss South Carolina State College.

I was born into a family of believers, educators and activists who served others, and blessed those who were less fortunate. Being the answered prayer of my ancestors and an example of a promising future are my lifelong goals of daily living.

As a beta club officer, cheerleader, student council officer, and Miss Jabberwock 1995 of the Greenwood Alumnae Chapter of Delta Sigma Theta Sorority, Inc.; after being sponsored by Ms Johnnie Posey, a loyal chapter member, and my youth mentor, my humble journey from a college girl to a college queen journey was framed by the Scripture, "I can do all things through Christ who strengthens me" (Philippians 4:13 NKJV).

It seems like it was just yesterday when my parents and I completed a whirlwind tour of their alma mater, Claflin University. At the conclusion, I inquired, "What school is that next door?" My mom quickly answered, "That's South Carolina State College. Why do you ask?" I later toured, applied, and the rest is history.

My experience at South Carolina State unequivocally gave me the confidence to be the master of my life, and the captain of my soul. Being crowned as Miss South Carolina State College and grafted into a lineage of black college queens of a culture, a cause, and a calling of giving back will forever be one of my greatest accomplishments.

My Journey to Miss SCSU

As freshmen girls, we were excited to attend the Miss South Carolina State College Pageant. We wanted to see what the excitement was all about.

"I want to be Miss SCSU when I am a senior," I said as we sat in the back of Henderson Davis Theatre. It was a four-year journey that allowed me to set a goal. During the campaign period, I requested the support of my Alpha Xi Chapter members of Delta Sigma Theta Sorority, Inc., my spring '88 Line Sisters (40 Signs of the Time), ROTC family, the SCSC Dancers whom I loved being a part of, my Williams Hall Sisters, and my fellow Professional English classmates.

My roommate and line sister Angela T. Clark, said, "Jones, we are going to make this happen." There were ten of us vying for the esteemed title. I was extremely nervous because one of the contestants was a native of Orangeburg and definitely no stranger to the campus. After speaking with my parents about my dream, they encouraged me to reach out to the alumnae of South Carolina State who lived in our hometown of Greenwood, South Carolina. The response was overwhelming. Many sent prayers and poems to encourage me. I also received pledges to help towards any expenses if I won. I was moved to tears throughout the entire process.

The campaign period was packed with opportunities to speak to the student body and at various assemblies. This time of my life was filled with positivity and sisterhood. No drama, no doubts. I am a firm believer that when women of purpose and promise come together, only great things can come from whatever the task may be.

On the night of the elections, I was in my room with my roommate, Bridgette Benbow. We were trying to act as if it was a normal night of conversation, while studying and preparing for the next day. It was everything but normal. We were preparing to head to the Student Center when I got a call from Tiger Rucker.

"Dee Dee, you won!" I cried like a newborn baby, then called my parents. They screamed for what seemed to be ten minutes. It will be a night I will never forget.

After I contacted all of my hometown supporters and shared news of our victory, I was blessed with donations that allowed me to purchase the dress I wanted. God is great and greatly to be praised. As I reflect on this journey, I can clearly see how He was preparing me to realize His tangible goodness, and power in my life.

My court was amazing. I actually shared the court with a home girl. Yes, two young ladies from "The Emerald City"—Greenwood, South Carolina, made history.

If you can believe it, you can achieve it. This mantra followed me right into planning and experiencing a beautiful coronation. Be Forever Yourself was the theme. I was super nervous because this was the first time since anyone could remember that Dr. Frank Mundy would not be available to choreograph and oversee the masterpiece of the SCSC Coronation. Remember what Angela said to me? Well, we made it happen. I am forever grateful for everyone who played a vital role in that magical evening. I am forever grateful to the advisor for Miss SCSU, Ms. Connie Shivers. Her love and sacrifice will always be appreciated.

My experience as a black College queen can be summed up in many, many ways. However, these words flood my mind as I think back: Special, humbling, fun, transformational, royal, epitome of excellence, magical, and unforgettable. Thank you SCSC! Bulldogs forever!

As we fast forward thirty-one years later, it is from the core of my experiences as an HBCU Queen that I served honorably in the United States Army as a Quartermaster Officer, a corporate leader with Phillip Morris Corporation, Bell South, Adecco Staffing, Avaya, Inc. and as an entrepreneur for sixteen years as CEO of Divine Cleaning Services, LLC, a full-service commercial service company. In July

2021, I established DD Jones Enterprise, LLC as a licensed insurance agent. I can hold my head high and thank God for using that time in my life to mold me into the woman I am today.

As a daughter, sister, wife, mother and now a "GrandDee" (Roman's grandmother), I can unquestionably see how God ordained this experience through the support of my angel like parents John and Joyce Jones. Their encouragement to be a college queen has left an imprint on my mind to dream, on my soul to excel, a resolve to accept God's perfect will, and a heart to love unconditionally, and without limits.

I have been blessed with two precious children: Taylor Nicole and Aaron LaBruce Horton, II. As I parent, I can emphatically relate to the sacrifices made for me by other working parents during my reign. In that spirit, I am determined to be an example to them of what it looks like to serve a God who is love, who is sovereign, and who is king. As a college queen, I learned to be diligent with demonstrating the golden rule, and living authentically with a dedicated mindset, heart set, and skill set that all things are possible if you *just believe*.

About Darcele Denise Jones-Horton "Dee Dee"

Darcele D. Jones-Horton (affectionately known as Dee Dee) is a native of Greenwood, South Carolina. She was educated in the public school system, and gleaned from great educators, leaders, and mentors; two of whom were her amazing parents Mamie B. Jones, and the late John Jones, Sr. Dee Dee grew up in a loving, and blessed home with the best family support system a woman could ask for. Dee Dee accepted Christ at the age of 13, and continues to walk in the power, and promises of God's unfailing love, and word. She earned a Bachelor of Arts Degree in Professional English, Cum Laude, from South Carolina State University in 1990, and served as a student body elected ambassador of the school as Miss South Carolina State University 1989-1990. Dee Dee served in the United States Army as a Quartermaster Officer until 1993. During her tenure as a consistent Top 10 Sales Agent with Bell Atlantic Nynex Mobile in Hartford, Connecticut, she earned a Masters of Science Degree, Magna Cum Laude, in Organizational Behavior from the University of Hartford in Hartford, Connecticut in 1998. Dee Dee has served exemplary in Corporate America with Louis Rich, Bellsouth, and Avaya, where she has earned numerous individual accolades, and team awards which all prepared her to step out on faith as an Entrepreneur in 2005. Dee Dee is the CEO of a Commercial and Residential Cleaning Company, Divine Cleaning Services, LLC for 16 years. In 2015 she earned her Life Insurance license, and recently formed her newest company, Dee Dee Jones Enterprises, LLC. she aspires to become a Million Dollar Producer, and Agency Builder and to pave the way for 100 women to do the same, and better over the next 10 years.

Dee Dee has a passion for serving, and encouraging God's kingdom through her roles as a mother, a community advocate for children in the school system, a youth ministry leader, prayer warrior, and a 33 year active member of Delta Sigma Theta Sorority Inc.

Dee Dee is a devoted mother of 2 children, Taylor and Aaron Horton, II, and a "Grand Dee" to her precious 2 year old grandson Roman Alexander Horton-White. Her favorite scripture is Philippians 4:13, "I can do all things through Christ who strengthens me."

RAVEEN CHILDS

Enter to Learn; Depart to Serve
Raveen Childs
Miss Morris College 2020-2021

As I entered the gates of Morris College in August of 2017, I knew I had found my home away from home. I knew there was the reason God brought me here. College recruiter Mr. Rivers came to my school and recruited students during my senior year. I already made my mind up that I was not attending Morris College. By the end of my senior year, I had a change of heart. Mr. Rivers came to my school again, and this time I applied. I was so excited because it was the first college application I completed. I went home and told my mom and my sister, Eboni Childs who was enrolled at Morris College at the time as Miss Homecoming. My god sister Alazia G. Williams also attended Morris College and served as the 64th Miss Morris College. A few weeks went by, and I received an acceptance letter. I was so excited. I was ready to go off to school, to decorate my dorm and meet my lifelong friends.

In August 2017, I was preparing for freshman orientation. I was up at 5 a.m., packing the car and ready to start my new journey at my new home for the next four years. Greeted by smiling faces and students ready to help, I knew I made the right choice. I found my home away from home. After the freshman move-in week, the first campaign was held for the title of Miss Freshman. I had so much faith that I would win. Just within a couple days, I made new friends and already had a reputation for always smiling around campus and talking to any and everyone just to make their day.

I was so nervous when the night of speeches for the title came. I've always been a talkative person; but to stand and speak in front of over 100 freshmen who were strangers to me, I was terrified! Alazia read over my speech several times to make sure it was perfect.

I thought the speech was perfect as well until the ballot was released. I did not win. Although I was very sad about it, I did not let that stop me. Once again, I knew it was a reason I was there.

Shortly after that, I was crowned Miss Amma Hall. During my sophomore year, I did not have a crown; but I was class president which was enough for me. I wanted to be the voice for my class so everyone could have the college experience they desired.

Fast forward to my senior year. I'd made it this far, and I knew it was my time. The campus held elections for the 67th Miss Morris College during the spring break of 2019. I was so excited that it was finally my time. I was campaigning from sunup to sundown. However, all of what we used to know at Morris was going to change. No more going to the cafeteria or sitting on the yard. No more sporting activities and no more being around those who I called my family for the last four years of my life. That was the start of the global pandemic. So, you were probably thinking exactly what I thought: *How I can represent my school virtually?*

I reached out to the person I thought always had the answer, Ms. Shakara "Nunu" Parks. As my pageant coach/choreographer, she inspired me so much since we first met. She told me that serving as Miss Morris College is more than just a title. My main mission was to leave my mark and be able to serve and represent my school virtually. Being the 2020-2021 Miss Morris College did not have all the "pomp and circumstance" that's usually associated with the title, but this year has not been like anything we have ever experienced before.

We have all had to adjust and adapt to a changing world. We've had to find new ways of learning, create new ways of achieving, build new ways to survive, and craft new ways to celebrate. Through the toil and turmoil of this past year, I have gained a deeper appreciation for my family, my friends and for Morris College. I know that the campus experience, the friendships I have formed, the guidance I have received and the push for academic success have all gotten me to this point and prepared me for future endeavors.

I take to heart our motto, "Enter to Learn; Depart to Serve." As I prepare for my next step, I would be remiss not to use my role to embolden and motivate my fellow peers. So, I would like to leave you with the words *uplift, nurture, inspire, transform* and *encourage*. These words make up my personal mantra and purpose for education: U.N.I.T.E., because united we stand, divided we fall.

Uplift-stay woke about today's society and how you can make a difference. Always remember that you are enough, and that intelligence is fashionable.

Nurture-your mind by striving for and achieving academic success. Malcom X once said, "Education is the passport to the future, for tomorrow belongs to those who prepare for it today."

Inspire-others are looking at you, make sure they are looking up. Your words and your actions have impact, make sure that it is positive.

Transform-be the change you want to see and don't live up to the stereotype.

Encourage-nothing is impossible; the word itself says "I'm possible."

About Raveen Childs

Ms. Raveen Childs, a native of Greenville, South Carolina, is the daughter of Mrs. Yalonda Childs and Mr. Eddie Childs. Raveen was born November 9,1999. She has 2 brothers and 2 sisters Sakira Childs, Alexander Childs, Eboni Childs and Carston Childs. Raveen is a recent graduate of the illustrious Morris College with a bachelors of fine arts in Mass Communications. Raveen joined the Morris College family in the fall of 2017. Aspiring to make a difference on campus, Raveen wanted to find a way to uplift others and invoke positivity and enthusiasm across the campus. She realized that the position as Miss Morris College would be more than an opportunity to be seen, but a chance to serve her institution and inspire Hornet Pride in her peers. With the support of her family and friends. Striving to excel in her academic, social, and civic pursuits, Raveen was actively invested in various clubs & organizations to include the Morris College Student Leaders,Student Ambassador, Student Government Association, Ladies of Morris, Morris College cheerleading and a member of Alpha Kappa Alpha Sorority Incorporated. Raveen entered into Morris to learn and as her time swiftly passed she will depart to serve. Raveen currently is working as a full time nail technician hoping to inspire other young people to take the leap of faith to become an entrepreneur. Raveen is also in the process of launching a plus size clothing boutique from sizes 14-20 called "PHAT GIRLZ" which stands for pretty, hot and thick letting all women know all shapes and sizes are beautiful plus the curves!

TANISHA FORDHAM

God Decides

TaNisha Fordham

Miss North Carolina A&T State University 2008-2009

"God uses the foolish things to confound the wise…" (1 Corinthians 1:27). This I know for sure. While I'm thankful for all that God has done in, around and through me (mostly in spite of myself), I must admit that I spend most of my time lost in the sauce.

A few months ago, I released my first feature documentary entitled, "Queen." We premiered at the Pan African Film and Arts Festival based in Los Angeles, California. PAFF is the largest black film festival in the entire world, but when you hear the trajectory of my life leading up to that moment, it's all very unconventional.

Hours after winning Miss North Carolina A&T State University, I was walking around campus and remember like it was yesterday a conversation that ensued:

"Hey, TaNisha."

A student approached me very informally. She wasn't someone who I considered a close friend, but she was someone that I knew from around campus and considered "friend-ish."

"Hey Danielle."

Her name has been changed to "Danielle" to protect her identity and the soon-to-be-mentioned nonsense that will now be her legacy.

"I'm proud of you girl…"

She stared before continuing…

"And, I just want you to know that you have my full support…"

In an instant, this moment suddenly became precious. Anyone who has ever tried to do something impactful and important I know will relate: the voices of those who are against you can so often seem so much louder than the voices of those who are for you. So, it's nice to feel supported.

"Danielle," was not a student who I would have assumed would vote for me during my campaign to become Miss A&T. Of course, I couldn't be sure without explicitly asking, but I would've assumed that "Danielle," had voted for one of the other candidates (both of whom, by the way, are beautiful human beings, one has since become a dear, dear friend—*just for the record*).

I am often the underdog. I am thankful to be ever present about the reality that it is never me and my "miraculousness" at work, but that it is God, in fact, at work in me. *I have no problem with that.* I have fully accepted that, "We have [our] treasure in earthen vessels to show that this surpassingly great treasure is of God and [is not] our own…" I am proud to be filled up with God's light. I hope I am honoring Him with it, but what that means is that people will often only see this vessel and forget that it's a broken jar, but it's filled with God's goodness.

I've always been told:

"You're too this…"

"You're too that…"

"Not quite this enough for this…"

"Not quite that enough for that…"

But I have tried desperately to attune my ear to God's voice and dismiss any voice that doesn't align with what He has said.

This particular day in 2008, only a few hours after being given the title of Miss North Carolina A&T State University, as I stood next to Murphy Hall (our student activities building at the time), I continued my ever-improving practice of ignoring the voices that didn't align with God's.

Just as I was fully giving into the precious nature of this moment, "Danielle" continued:

"So… I know that now that you're Miss A&T and headed to the Miss HBCU pageant, you're likely going to start focusing more on your weight and appearance. And, I can help you girl—*I got you.*"

Was this girl calling me fat?

Was she saying that I couldn't dress?

Was she calling me fat?

Danielle smiled politely, which only further confused me. She looked into my eyes and forged ahead.

"Seriously girl, I mean it… I'm very into working out and eating right—*I can get you on a plan.* And, we can go shopping together; I'll get you together… *I won't let you be out here looking crazy…*"

I.

WON'T.

LET YOU.

BE OUT HERE—

LOOKING...

CRAZY

.

.

.

I stared.

I smiled.

I blinked.

I breathed deeply.

I sighed.

I inhaled. I exhaled. I inhaled.

Time slowed for just a few moments, *and then* I said the only thing that came to mind:

"Thanks, girl. I appreciate you. Yeah, I'll reach out…"

But I never ended up reaching out because "Danielle's" opinion didn't matter. I wasn't elected by the "Danielles" of the world. "Danielle" hadn't called me to freshmen class presidency or sophomore class presidency. "Danielle" hadn't gotten me on the radio my sophomore and junior years. "Danielle" hadn't called me to produce a talk show for local television my junior and senior years at A&T and, when I went to compete for Miss HBCU (Miss National Black College Alumni Hall of Fame), "Danielle" wasn't responsible for my ultimate win of that title *either*.

I was a bit beset, of course. "Danielle's" flippant disregard for the sanctity of my—self, her inability to see that I was more than just a body, clothes and hair, and her ultimate assessment that I would need to conform to her standard in order to be counted or impactful really hurt. Yes, I am not an alien. I am not extraterrestrial. That comment stung, and it stung badly. But ultimately, I took that sting, I licked my wounds and I kept marching because I was keenly aware that God had called me to that post, and He had a plan for many other posts in my future.

There is a "Danielle" in every story. If the truth be told, sometimes we are our own "Danielle." There's always going to be some person or obstacle standing in your way, but I am confident in this: *God decides*. "Man makes plans, but it is God who establishes every step." That was my experience while campaigning for and eventually serving as Miss A&T and HBCU and that has been my life's story.

The noise makers aren't going to stop making noise.

Even in the moments in your life where you should be the happiest, there's always going to be someone waiting with a needle to poke a hole in your balloon to deflate you just a bit, but God decides. When I competed for Mrs. New Jersey United States in 2019, I had a similar experience. There was a lot of discussion around me being the first potential Mrs. New Jersey United States with sisterlocks. Was I refined enough? Was I poised enough, and on and on—but *God decided*. When I went on to compete for Mrs. United States, though I only placed Top 11; I was voted, "The People's Choice" in an online competition because even when man thinks he decided, God has the last say.

And, this isn't a pageantry specific message. This isn't a note for kings and queens (exclusively); this is a message for humankind.

I'll never forget that long drive from Phoenix, Arizona to Buffalo, New York in 2017.

I had all-of-the-sudden begun a fierce battle with anxiety and I was completely overwhelmed. I had never had a mental health battle before. I felt scared. I felt broken. I felt empty. I felt hopeless. I remember feeling so sad and confused.

"God, I've done so much in love and reverence for you. I've tried to live my whole life in honor of you. Why is this happening to me?"

I couldn't believe that life was forcing my husband and I back to the east coast. I couldn't breathe in Arizona. I don't know why, but I knew that I needed to get back close to home and family back on the east coast. There's no way that I could've known at that moment what I know now—a beautiful life, with much more joy than I ever could've imagined was waiting for me here. More love. More light. More friends. More time with family. More opportunities. More joy. More time with God. More of an understanding of the *true meaning* of life. I couldn't have forecast that, but here I am:

I am now the co-producer of an Oscar nominated film, a former Mrs. New Jersey United States, and the director and producer of a play that will open off-off Broadway in just a few months. But *more importantly*, I am a teacher, a mentor, a friend and *most importantly*, I am a daughter, a dog-mom, a wife and a child of God. And, if my year as Miss A&T taught me anything, it taught me this:

"We press to take hold of that for which Christ has taken hold of us." Life is gonna do what life is gonna do. But no matter what life looks like, no matter what "Danielle" is standing in front of you, no matter how big or scary or overwhelming the obstacle, God decides. And, God has a good, good, good, good, good, good plan for your life. So, all will be well.

About TaNisha Fordham

TaNisha Fordham, co-producer of the 2018 Oscar Nominated film, "My Nephew Emmett," is a writer, director, producer, performer, educator, and creative who, in 2019, was honored to have served as Mrs. New Jersey United States. Additionally, Fordham recently completed a residency with Rutgers University and their Express Newark CMC (filmmakers) Program, as well as a Director's Intensive with Steven Broadnax III with Roundabout Theater (Broadway).

Fordham has written, directed, and produced over 40 original productions, spanning several mediums, over the past 14 years through her company (www.enlightenedvisions.org). This year she had her feature - documentary, directorial debut, with, "Queen," which premiered at the Pan-African Film Festival (the largest international festival featuring stories that pan the African diaspora) which later (May 2021) won Most Inspirational Documentary at the International Christian Film Festival in Orlando, Florida. Fordham is super excited about her newest production, "12 Mo' Angry Men," (an adaptation of the widely known, "12 Angry Men," by Reginald Rose) which premiered as the City of Newark's first ever Theater in the Park production, the city's first city-sponsored theater production of its kind. Written, directed, produced by and starring Fordham, "12 Mo' Angry Men," is also scheduled to be workshopped at the 2021 "Winterfest," at the Latea Theater of Manhattan, and is also being considered by the Bishop Arts Theater of Dallas, Texas.

Fordham also has strong community ties across the nation. In 2020/21 she served on the Diversity, Equity and Inclusion committee at Bergen County Theater, hosting their first-ever DEI Town Hall. Additionally, in 2020 (immediately before the pandemic) Fordham gladly coordinated a CO-OP with the Pan-African Film and Arts Festival of LA providing students in NJ with the opportunity to travel across the country and work with the festival. Additionally, Fordham recently participated as an ensemble member at The Goodman Theater, of Chicago, in their "InterGens," program which lifts the voices of a diverse and intergenerational group of creatives.

Fordham has the distinct honor of being an educator, and in addition to her various creative endeavors, Fordham is committed to her theater and film students at Newark Collegiate Academy in Newark, New Jersey where Fordham serves as the Associate Art Director – Fordham considers her work in education to be some of the most sacred work that she is privileged to do.

Tea's mom: Pam, hubby: Rob, dog: Scoop, and grandparents: Freddie and Monte are her biggest inspirations and Jesus Christ is at the center of all she does.

Fordham would love to continue to build community with diverse communities around the nation and world — she prides herself in being accessible and super eager to connect: tanisha.fordham@gmail.com | www.enlightenedvision.org

CHINNA MAPP

For She That Endures Until the End
Chinna Mapp
Miss Claflin University 1997-1998

I vividly recall the smell of fresh cut grass as I moved into position on the walk to Moss Auditorium. The warm South Carolina sun gently kissed my face as I walked proudly amongst my peers all dressed in white for the matriculation day ceremony. We walked one by one, across the stage as our names, hometowns and majors were announced to a room full of university faculty and staff, as well as family and friends. All students had candles that were lit before crossing and those candles were extinguished upon reaching the opposite side of the stage. I entered Claflin symbolically clothed in white, and left Claflin dressed in a black cap and gown, which is customary of the lettered college graduate. However, it was a journey that I almost did not finish.

Between entering college as a freshman and exiting with my Bachelor of Science five years later, one of the most inspiring, yet enduring, things I experienced at Claflin was being crowned Miss Claflin 1997-1998. I believe there's no greater honor than someone choosing you to represent them.

Twice in my life, I've felt the need to be a voice for my community: once when I decided to participate in the Miss Claflin pageant to represent the student body and when I ran for office in the National Black Graduate Student Association. I think it was the community coming alive in me.

I've always had a passion for social justice and doing what is right for others, no matter what. I think this passion stemmed from my humble childhood and my own experiences of being made to feel less than during my middle school and part of my high school years. These experiences may be the reason why I always strive toward leaving people, places, things and situations better than I find them. My aim is to help others by making them feel comfortable and valued.

I am always curious about people. I really mean it when I ask, "How are you doing?" I anticipate an answer. I am not focused on what they do for a living. I'm focused on finding common ground by creating a safe space for us to connect as children of God.

My journey to being crowned college campus queen began as separate paths that converged in my decision to run for Miss Claflin. My path first started with a local Jabberwock pageant I participated in while I was in high school. I attended practice fifteen miles from my home in Neeses, South Carolina to a neighboring small town called Denmark. Mrs. Annette Albert not only opened her lovely home to the girls participating in the pageant, but she also made sure that I was transported to and from practice because my mom didn't have a car at that time. Even though I didn't win the pageant, the experience exposed me to other talented young women, and I developed a deeper appreciation for pageantry and fundraising. Through Mrs. Albert's acts of kindness, the love for performing, fundraising, commitment, and the value of community and communication, found their way into my heart.

The other path involved my introduction to what would come to be my beloved alma mater during my sophomore year at Hunter-Kinard-Tyler (HKT) High School. On a cold Wednesday in January, I was introduced to a village that would help raise me in more ways than one. Two representatives from then Claflin College, Ms. Shirley Ann Hugee and Mr. Leroy C. Fogle, whom I would later affectionately refer to as "LC," came to introduce HKT students to the Upward Bound Program, a national college-prep program housed at historically black colleges and universities.

This program aimed to help minority students become first-generation college graduates. After completing my application through our school counselor, Mr. Newsome, I was required to take an entrance exam in Claflin's historic Tingley Hall. I was accepted into the program and had to attend Saturday classes and summer classes during my junior and senior years. It is interesting how the things we seek equality for today were looked upon as normal during that time, especially by those who were on the receiving end. I probably would not have gone to Claflin if not for the Upward Bound Program, and the aid of LC and program director Mrs. Gwendolyn B. Phillips. These people were part of the village I did not know I needed. However, I am so grateful I had them during those trying years, although I seemed intent on disappointing them.

When I entered Claflin College as a freshman in 1994, I was already familiar with the campus. However, I was not familiar with what it took to be a successful college student. During my first year of college, I worked as a live-in nanny for a high school principal whose home was beyond walking distance from the campus. With no financial support from home, it was necessary for me to have income to support myself. I cooked, cleaned, and made sure that the kids got to school alright. I also helped the kids with their schoolwork and ensured that they had ample social and recreational activity. I was not the best nanny to Toni and Rocky, but I was an even worse student.

I didn't have a car. Living on the opposite side of town with no ride made getting to school somewhat difficult. My circumstances made me choose a job over my education, and I paid the price with an atrocious GPA at the end of my freshman year. Added to this dynamic was the fact that my then boyfriend was stationed in Japan. My teenaged selfishness overrode my better judgment and missing him prompted me to make overseas calls that resulted in a ridiculously high telephone bill for my employer. I had to face the consequences and pay for the calls I made. My employer was gracious about it, but it was a clear example of how youth can limit your perspective at times.

Fortunately, my village came to my rescue. The Upward Bound director pulled me into her office for a stern talking before offering salvation in the form of an on-campus job. This job would help me financially and provide free housing in the college dormitory. I gave back as much as I could by mentoring the young women under my charge while balancing school and working additional jobs for the purpose of attending to my family's needs. I worked in post office and bookstore on campus. Every other weekend, I worked as a CNA during the weekends, and I did my best to juggle cheerleading practice and basketball games. Entering a college pageant was the last thing on my mind … until I saw it as an opportunity to be a voice for the student body.

I faced my fears and competed against others who I felt at the time were smarter, prettier, and more heavily favored to win than I was. I eventually realized that for myself and other young women aspiring to be queens, one must first realize that you *already are* a queen. This may take some convincing, but you must know that beautiful jewelry, clothing, makeup, physical alterations and enhancements, designer clothes and particular affiliations do not make you a queen. You are a queen because, despite your beliefs or practices, you have been blessed with God-given talents. You can use them to make the community you serve a better place for all.

In today's post-pandemic learning environment, classrooms may be virtual; but they are still a shared space. There is room to learn, grow and operate in love and kindness. Follow the Golden Rule: "Do unto others as you would have them do unto you." Take time to ask yourself questions about what you want for your life. More importantly, respond to those questions and chart a course toward whatever actions that help you realize your goals.

Frequently look back and celebrate your accomplishments. Learn to give yourself credit for what you've done, even when others do not. Know your worth. Learn everything that you honestly can. It's so easy to find virtual hacks and answers to life's mysteries. Learn to answer questions for yourself first, and then go seeking. It's important to adopt your own perspective and not let social media and/or friends to dictate your response to anything. This is how you develop your own voice and know who you really are.

My journey seemingly began as two separate paths that converged beautifully when I was crowned Miss Claflin College 1997-98. I wanted to serve as a queen who did not take herself too seriously, but instead took seriously the work of being a student ambassador. I hope that the student body members who matriculated with me experienced less of a divide and more of an unspoken feeling that communicated we are all in this together.

It all made sense once I was crowned Miss Claflin. Even though I was standing there, Charles, Sr. and Peggie Davis, Keiotha, Beionka, Latasha, and Charles Jr., Renell, the Jenkins family, Bushy Pond Baptist Church family, the Johnson family, the Williams Family, Mr. and Mrs. Albert, Mr. Newsome, Ms. Hugee, Mrs. Phillips, Mr. Fogle, my line sisters, my cheerleading squad members, Carla, Tara, Trisa, Shica, Karen, Ja'Kia, Dee, Mrs. Kelly, Emily, the students, staff, my church ... they were all there with me. I could not have achieved any of the things that I did without them. My being crowned was a culmination of all of their acts of kindness and support. When I stood to be crowned, I stood *with* them and *for* them. When I bowed, I bowed to them because truly, I was humbled, blessed and undeserving; yet, they saw something in me that I did not see. They believed in me enough to say, "Yes! We choose you to represent us."

My community lifted me up and allowed me to serve them. I see no greater honor than that.

About Chinna Mapp

Chinna Deionne Mapp (nee Davis) has built a career as an educator that has allowed her to use her talents in rural, urban and international school districts.

Born in Jefferson Parish in Louisiana, Chinna spent a few years in Oakland, California before landing in Neeses, South Carolina. It is here that she found her passion for sports and pageantry. At Hunter-Tyler Kinnard high school she found time to participate in softball, basketball and volleyball all the while cheering from the sidelines as a cheerleader.

China enrolled in the Upward Bound program at then Claflin College and spent her weekends and summers engaged in enriching academic and social activities that planted the seed that would grow into a keen interest in attending Claflin.

While at Claflin, Chinna majored in Biology while still finding time to endear herself to her peers, becoming a leading member of the Claflin College Cheerleading squad, a member of the Gamma Chi Chapter of Delta Sigma Theta Sorority, Inc. and being crowned Miss Claflin University 1997-1998.

After graduating from Claflin in 1999 and a brief time at her high school alma mater, she became a Wildland Fire Fighter with Savannah River Site in New Ellenton, South Carolina before going back to the classroom in Richmond, Virginia. After taking a two-year sabbatical to acquire a Master of Science degree in Biology, she went on to teach in the Washington DC/Maryland area before going abroad to teach in 2015.

Chinna has been married to Travis Mapp for 14 years. They have two sons: Ahmad, 10 and Ibrahim, 8. They currently live and work in the United Arab Emirates.

FAITH RENEÉ SPELLS

A Girl named Faith, with Alopecia
How Becoming Miss Voorhees College
Assisted Me Accepting My True Self

Faith Reneé Spells

Miss Voorhees College 2002-2003

Here I was.

A girl named Faith, just finding out that I won the title of Miss Voorhees College, 2002-2003. I honestly did not expect to win. Even though I was no stranger to the pageantry life, I was still in initial shock of winning this title. I've held titles before, from being named Miss Senior at Edisto High School to being named Miss Freshman of Voorhees College. Yet, even with the many titles, accomplishments or winnings, I felt undeserving of them. I unknowingly held many insecurities within myself, primarily that of being an *alopecian.*

What is an alopecian? An alopecian is a person who has experienced minimal or extreme hair loss. I was diagnosed with the most extreme type of alopecia, *alopecia universalis.* This diagnosis meant that I had experienced between 80-100% of hair loss on my body. Being one of the six-plus million people diagnosed with this auto-immune deficiency, I've dealt with the stares, the bullying and the insecurity of being a bald woman.

How could I be a queen? Would I not be made fun of, or bullied due to my shortcomings? Who would see me as a queen—a *bald* queen at that? However, winning the title of Miss Voorhees not only laid the foundation of me accepting myself, but also embracing my differences and blessings.

Yes, *blessings*.

Since age four, I've always felt isolated, excluded nor a part of the "in crowd" due to my hair loss. One time, a classmate thought it would be funny to put glue in my wig. Talk about utter embarrassment and sadness that I endured that day. Another time, I was bullied during school lunch break for being "Ms. Clean."

Being named the queen of the college catapulted me in accepting and embracing my many differences and blessings in my hair loss. Not only was I the college's queen, but I was also a passionate stylist/braider on campus. Upon graduation, I often wondered how my coronation would have been different if I had chosen to be "my authentic self."

Fast forward to the year of 2013, nearly ten years later. That year, I decided that I would not only hold the title of queen but embrace my inheritance of the title. That was the year that I revealed my secrets—my struggles with insecurities, depression and self-esteem. That was the year that I launched "Alopecian Beauty," my social media handle on most outlets.

The term "Alopecian Beauty" embodies the royalty of a queen who displays the uniqueness of her bald and bold beauty. Never in a thousand years did I expect the "acceptance" nor the acknowledgement of many women and men who had the same condition. To become free from something that seemingly held you hostage or bound for many years, was a sweet release.

One of my favorite scriptures is Hebrews 11:1 KJV, "Now faith is the substance of things hoped for, the evidence of things not seen."

I truly believe and feel that this Scripture sums up the years of my livelihood.

As I embraced my truths, I was not only able to be free, but I assisted other women in the process to express their own level of freedom and self-worth. From being a speaker at a conference in Houston, Texas, to being an attributing author to a book, to being invited to speak at other engagements and women's conferences, I fully embraced and embodied Alopecian Beauty.

My greatest joy was being a beacon of light for not only the young girls, but even the seasoned women in my life who felt alone or even ashamed of their hair loss. It was a beautiful blessing to identify with someone whom you feel like "yourself" around. Assisting women to understand their self-worth and value all began at the inception of being named Miss Voorhees College. While the manifestation of the blessing and gift took time, as I myself embraced Faith, it was well worth it.

2020 not only took away many things from us—even perhaps our loved ones, but for those of us who are fortunate, we were blessed with the time, space and opportunity to embrace each other, learn each other and make countless memories with each other.

During 2020, I reflected on how much different my platform would have been if I had embraced my truths versus running away from them.

So, I with that thought, allow me to encourage someone. Whatever "message" or "gift" the Most High has blessed you with, do not sit on it. Get up and get to moving. Spread your wings and embrace your truths. After all, someone is waiting on that particular "word" that will give them a breath of fresh air into their lives.

- Do not sit on your uniqueness.

- Do not sit on your divine visions.

- Do not dismiss those "God winks."

- Do not allow fear to discount the promises made to and for you.

- Do not allow another person's experience to rob you of yours.

- Do not forfeit your future because your present is not what you want it to be.

- Do not allow the "stages of your life" to make you dismiss the promises for your life.

As a girl named Faith, who has alopecia, you and your story matters.

As a queen who has alopecia, you and your unique beauty mark makes a difference.

As a queen named Faith, I am here to remind you that life does get better.

Whether you have experience alopecia or not, whatever vices that you have or will experience in life, not matter what—keep moving. If I had decided to continue down the path of being destructive towards my own life due to my lack of hair, depression and insecurity, I would not be able to pen any words that you're reading right now.

While you may never contemplate suicide or have manic depressive thoughts, just know that your thoughts have power—just as the words you speak have power. Even if you've never dealt with any level of insecurities, still be kind, as we all are fighting with something. Be kind because we all are experiencing or will encounter some level of change in our lives. Whether or not you choose to run and compete for a title, never neglect the ultimate title of understanding the importance of your *self-worth*.

If I could rewind the hands of time, I would have had the confidence and willpower to embrace "Faith." I would have the pictures of my crown glistening upon my perfectly molded bald head. Yet, since it is impossible to do so, allow me the opportunity to assist you in ensuring that your "crown" is not tilting nor completely off.

Hold your head up. Square your shoulders back. Wipe your tears if you should, and cry again if you need to; but after all is said and done, straighten your crown and know that you are not only a part of a royal family and priesthood, but you are beautifully and wonderfully made in the image of the Most High God.

While our paths may never cross other than you reading the words within this chapter, know that not only am I rooting for you to win, but I am also sincerely praying for and with you.

Crowns Up!

Your Alopecian Beauty

About Faith Reneé Spells

Faith Reneé Spells, brings you greetings from Cordova, SC. An Alumni of Voorhees College, class of 2003; she completed her Bachelor of Science degree in Computer Science while serving as Miss Voorhees College 2002-2003.

During her time at Voorhees; Faith also was involved with the following organizations: The Theta Epsilon Chapter of Zeta Phi Beta Sorority, Inc., Elizabeth Evelyn Wright Theater Guild, Science Club, SGA, Pre-Alumni Association, along with many others.

Upon completing her Bachelor's Degree, she accepted the call into ministry in 2004; where she was license to preach the unadulterated truth of Jesus Christ.

In addition, Faith has received two MBA degrees with a concentration in Business Administration and Human Resources, respectively, from Colorado Technical University.

As woman of God who is for the people of God; she is God's servant for such a time as this. Above all of her educational endeavors and community service accolades; her greatest joy is being able to minister to person's who is seeking Jesus in these last days and times.

She is currently employed at Denmark Technical as the College Registrar. An advocate for the arena of education, Faith has over 16 years of experience in student advocacy, registration, admissions, enrollment management and advising.

In her spare time, Faith wears many hats also: a sin mother, a passionate stylist, motivational speaker, poet, an aspiring author, and above all else, one who is chasing after God's own heart. Her favorite scripture is Hebrews 11: 1- "Now Faith is the substance of things hoped for and the evidence of things not yet seen."

Faith currently resides in Orangeburg, SC with her one year old son, Sir Grayson.

JADA BROWN

Purpose, Persistence, Prosperity

Jada Brown

Miss North Carolina A&T State University 2018-2019

*"When purpose is present, nothing can stop
a determined individual's rendezvous with destiny."*

Born and raised in Columbia, South Carolina, I've always had a drive and passion to learn and try new things. The day I was born, right after my twin sister, I turned around and took 45 minutes to arrive into the world. Sometimes, I think I've always had a natural tendency to second guess myself. That hesitation has stuck with me throughout many of my life's decisions, but I have always been able to prosper. Despite being a "late bloomer" at almost everything, I've always had the capacity to lead and work hard, whether it was making straight A's in school or participating in several extracurricular activities, starting with my first love, basketball. However, I knew my shooting guard days were over as I became a teenager and entered into the fine art of dance. I loved performing different genres of dance such as ballet, jazz, liturgical, mime, hip hop and even African. Beyond that, I developed a love for the art of stepping. I loved competing with my school's teams and performing in community shows.

After serving as co-captain for some time and later being denied the position of captain on my high school's step team, I began to doubt my ability to lead. With these gifts, I also faced a new challenge of having fallen arches in my feet, which ultimately made it difficult to perform. However, hope wasn't all lost. I was introduced to a new confident lifestyle that elevated not only my self-esteem, but my arches and height, too!

Modeling was a new talent and craft that came along once I stopped playing sports and dancing slowed down. Although I've always involved myself with youth fashion shows, I've never thought that I would cross over into the professional spectrum of the fashion world. In high school, I got my first real opportunity to audition for Barbizon Talent & Modeling Agency training. Eventually, I signed with ICE Agency. I was offered the chance to go to a showcase in Miami. I opened up the big show right behind a recent model from the legendary *America's Next Top Model*, wearing a huge designer's new collection. Scouts hand-picked certain girls to open in a designer's clothes in the beginning of the show. After a performance well done, I got callbacks after that show to meet the designers and agencies who participated as judges.

One of the first tables I was instructed to go to was the designer I wore opening the show. I was so excited to meet him and discuss my potential and future. I was asked what item from the collection I wore. After I described the dress, he mentioned how I had a great look and walk, but how the scouts should not have put me in that particular item. He explained how his dress was too tight around my hips and thighs, and that it was not a good fit. That excitement I once felt in that moment suddenly disappeared, knowing I opened the show and was not the best fit to represent the design. *Was I enough?*

After that embarrassing moment, I soon discovered the other callback with another agency's table and that is when I met Mr. Lyndon, who represented HOP Models & Talent Agency based in Atlanta and Chicago. Having been hesitant after presenting my portfolio and having a one on one, he reassured me that my size, height and features were all enough to be signed. I had a new confidence and was reminded of the black excellence that I represented on that stage. I signed on to a professional contract and booked my first photoshoot in Georgia. I began to travel, do shows and auditions in the fashion industry. I also went on to compete in my first pageant, and I became Miss Congeniality, Miss Junior, and Miss Ridge View High School. Even though I won, the decision to compete was something I did for my friend to replace her because she dropped out due to personal concerns. Was I really a queen?

Singing was another talent that the late Monica Jackson helped me discover, even if that meant crying throughout my first church solo. She showed me that there was a beautiful soprano way down inside that was waiting to be heard outside of the youth choir section.

In high school, my twin sister Jenai, my friends Whitney and Brittani, and I went on to create a gospel group called the "Righteous Pearls." We rehearsed almost every day after school, preparing for events. We had auditions for school events such as the Black History Month program and senior assembly. We even auditioned to sing the national anthem at our graduation, landing each one. Righteous Pearls got our first big opportunity after we sang Destiny's Child's rendition of the national anthem for our high school graduation. A news reporter was outside interviewing students and decided to put me and my sister on TV after the graduation. The reporter asked for our contact information so we could get our own segment on the local news. We got our band and selections together, and we performed for our first big moment. Not long after this, it was time for us all to go to college. I would soon have to find and walk in the purpose God had for me. I left to attend the illustrious North Carolina Agricultural & Technical State University.

At the open house, I was surely excited for the fall semester. Over the summer through Twitter, I met who would now be my lifelong best friend, Blaike Bibbs, another incoming freshman to A&T. I gained mentors from the Columbia, SC North Carolina A&T Alumni Chapter who helped my transition into college. Having learned my background, the chapter president looked me in my eyes and told me I was going to be their next Miss North Carolina A&T.

When I met Blaike on campus, she even told me her mom saw me at an open house, pointed me out and said I looked like I would be a Miss NC A&T, not knowing me and her daughter would one day become best friends. Finding my way through freshman and sophomore year, I joined the modeling troop *Couture*, the praise dancers of the NC A&T Fellowship Gospel Choir, SC Aggies, Ladies of Excellence, honor societies, and psychology department organizations. I soon discovered an organization of women joined and became their queen.

100 Collegiate Women was an organization that grew to 400+ members. Coming onto their eBoard was my first big opportunity on campus where I felt I could be impactful. My transparency and leadership skills gave other young women permission to show up more authentically, and not hide behind their gifts or flaws. Spearheading programs such as "Head over Heels" reminded the ladies of the campus to walk in confidence with their best foot forwards. Additionally, I organized an annual program to honor the men of the campus called "Kings Appreciation." It was the first time the campus had seen the women of Aggieland come together to highlight men on campus, and to show love, encouragement and support. I was also encouraged by my group of friends to run for Junior Class Secretary to get into the Student Government Association. At first, I was hesitant because I did not think I was fit to do a campaign. Nevertheless, my support system insisted that I get out there, so the "Signed, Sealed, Delivered, I'm Yours!" campaign was birthed.

Competing only against a gold squad cheerleader at the time, some people doubted me. God saw fit for me to be elected for this position and proved to me what I could do. However, there was one thing that stood out. When most people saw me going for secretary, I was constantly asked why I was not running for a queen position. So many people told me they felt I had more inside, but I still didn't see it. During my junior year, there were student government interest meetings, and then there was the night the application for Miss NC A&T was due. Earlier that day, I took a nap, and my grandmother came to me in my dream.

"Queen, there's no need to continue to run; it's your time," my grandmother said to me in my dream. Even in that confirmation, I still hesitated; but I knew then that I had to be obedient. I was in tears, knowing that I had been running away from this; but at some point, God will position you to where you will have to fall on your knees.

I continued to doubt myself, leading up to the hours of the application's time to close. Then, I finally prayed and repeated my grandmother's words to myself: "You are a queen. It's your time!" Before I knew it, I pressed submit, not realizing what I had just done. I nervously called my mom and told her what I did. Excited, she immediately wanted to prepare. In two hours, my truth was revealed, and my platform was created: "Purpose, Persistence, Prosperity: Walking in Your Purpose, Maintaining Persistence, Achieving Prosperity." The pageant night, all of the things I had been involved in over the years including all of the self-doubts, paid off for that moment on the stage. My opening line was, "Whenever you look back on tonight's mix, think of me—your contestant number six!"

There were eight young ladies in total, vying to be the next Miss NC A&T State University, the largest group the campus had seen in some years. After walking away with the highest score from the pageant, and competing in a very competitive campaign season, I was crowned the 84th Miss North Carolina Agricultural and Technical State University. Soon came the reign and as a resilient queen, I truly learned the lesson of loving what you do in spite of what you feel. As the face of NC A&T, I always wanted to represent my Aggie community with my best and demonstrate the black excellence that HBCUs produce, which my parents had been my foundational example of.

I learned to prioritize the needs of the community versus my own vision. At that time, Greensboro was experiencing a big food insecurity. I partnered with Hot Dish & Hope and provided student volunteers to feed the homeless of our community. I was also afforded the opportunity to compete in the National Black College Alumni Hall of Fame pageant, where I placed in the top ten. I later went on to judge pageants such as a campus pageant for Miss Men on the Move, and the Atlantic Seaboard Beauty Pageant North Carolina Regional. I had the opportunity to be showcased in a fashion show with a former Miss USA, hosted by The Links, Inc. Also, I have worked with brands such as HBCU Pulse and HBCU Pride Nation.

My greatest honor in my reign involved another HBCU, Bennett College, which is one of only two all-women's HBCUs. It was time for the annual Ebony HBCU Campus Queen Competition. As a leader of the number one public HBCU, I felt that it was my duty to highlight the concerns of Bennett College possibly losing its accreditation and closing their doors. Bringing notice to this versus asking for votes for self-gain seemed more logical. The same number of votes and posts going towards the competition is the same amount of effort that I felt the community should be putting towards trying to keep our HBCU doors open.

My sister queen and former Miss Bennett College, Brooke Kane, did not have an opportunity to promote the Ebony competition, as her school's closing was more relevant. I noticed how often she posted about it and how so many others were not aware. Over the winter break, I made a video to post on social media highlighting this issue and forfeited the Ebony competition. I announced I was donating my votes from the competition to Miss Bennett College, someone who had represented herself in the time of adversity as a true queen. If anyone deserved a chance to be selected in that competition, she deserved it. Some might've felt it was a rebellious move, since no Miss A&T had ever pulled out of this competition; but in my heart and as a queen, I knew that was what I should do.

Soon after, my petition was drafted, emails were sent and I had several other HBCU queens following suit, leaving the competition. A new movement and a bigger push towards fundraising to keep Bennett College's doors open was sparked. Seeing that everyone came together and the HBCU community continued to push, Bennett College still stands, and this was a rewarding way to end my reign.

After my reign as Miss A&T, many doors were opened. After graduating with my bachelor's in psychology, I relocated to Maryland near the DC area. That's where I took my first corporate opportunity working for an educational technology company, 2U, Inc. I hesitated about moving from the south, but in just these short few years I have gained so much. Even being seven hours away from home, I still feel like I never left.

Being Miss A&T opened the door for speaking engagements with brands such as DC NOW Events and Dean Talk with Dr. Woodson to discuss leadership and the reign of a queen as a leader in the HBCU community. HBCU royalty opened many doors and formed many relationships that continues to propel me forward. Now, I'm pursuing my second degree at another HBCU, Bowie State University, to receive my master's degree in mental health counseling to become a licensed therapist.

There is no limit to the black excellence that HBCUs produce. I cannot wait to pour into the minds of the generations of tomorrow. As I am writing this during these unpredictable times in the year of 2021, I've faced life's hiccups, deaths, doubts and even depression; but I still have purpose. Through my persistence, I have purchased my first car this year, currently enrolled in an outstanding master's program, and now I can add author to my resume. Jeremiah 29:11 NIV says, *"For I know the plans I have for you," declares the LORD, "plans to prosper you and not harm you, plans to give you hope and a future."* Everything I went through was according to God's purpose for me, and I have felt the prosperity of it all.

So, I say to you, what is your purpose? Will you remain persistent? If you do, you will surely prosper.

About Jada Alaina Brown

For the 2018-2019 academic school year, Miss Jada Alaina Brown reigned as the 84th Miss North Carolina Agricultural and Technical State University; on the platform, Purpose, Persistence, Prosperity: Walking In Your Purpose, Maintaining Persistence, and Achieving Prosperity. Hailing all the way from Columbia, South Carolina, her desire was to help the University to continue to evolve and thrive by strengthening the "Aggie" community both on and off campus. Jada believes that everyone has a purpose and that her God-given purpose is to help others.

Jada has been on the Dean's List every semester since her Freshman year and is a member of Alpha Lambda Delta National Honor Society, Psi Chi Honor Society, and the Alpha Kappa Mu Honor Society. She was also actively involved in several organizations on her campus. She has served as the 2017-2018 Junior Class Secretary, the Psychology Research Club, the South Carolina Aggies Organization, the Ladies of Excellence, and for a term, she served as a praise dancer with the University's Gospel Choir. During the 2017-18 academic year, Jada also served as Miss 100 Collegiate Women. Through all of these organizations, Jada has been dedicated to helping others through volunteerism and community service. Jada has had pageantry experience through achieving titles such as Miss Congeniality, Miss Junior, and Miss Ridge View High in the Miss Ridge View High School Pageant of 2014. She also was a finalist in the Miss North Carolina A&T State University Pageant of 2018, and had the honor of placing in the Top Ten in the National Black College Alumni Hall of Fame Pageant in Atlanta, Georgia in September of 2018.

Jada has her bachelor's degree in Psychology and is a proud graduate of the class of 2019 from the illustrious North Carolina

Agricultural and Technical State University. Jada started her professional career in the student engagement department for 2U Inc., an educational technology company that partners with top colleges and universities to bring their degree programs and credit-bearing courses online.

Jada plans to further her education at Bowie State University to receive her masters degree in Mental Health Counseling. In her personal time, she loves to network, enjoys brunch in the city, loves to dance and sing, model, give back to the community and create new memories with family and friends.

Each day, Jada steps out on her faith with one of her favorite scriptures always at the forefront in her mind which says, *"For I know the plans I have for you," declares the Lord, "plans to prosper you and not to harm you, plans to give you hope and a future."* (Jeremiah 29:11, NIV)

DARBY SMITH

088.

Darby Smith

Miss Southern University and A&M 2018-2019

I never saw myself becoming Miss Southern University. I always knew that I was going to attend Southern University. I come from a family of "jaguars." My mom met my dad at Southern; my aunt met my uncle at Southern and my sister also graduated from Southern. I had attended every Bayou Classic in New Orleans every Thanksgiving Weekend since age fifteen. Everybody that's attended SU has college stories to last a lifetime. I am a two-time Graduate of Southern University with a B.S. in Marketing and an M.P.A., from Shreveport, La.

I saw my first Miss Southern University at my freshman orientation. She was so poised and well spoken. HBCU royalty seemed like another world from where I was. I walked back to my dorm with a group of suitemates and roommates. We all talked about our aspirations--what we wanted to be at Southern, where we wanted to go, and what we wanted to accomplish. One friend said that she knew confidently she was going to be Miss Southern University, another, a class Queen. As I listened to my friends talk about their aspirations, I was just happy to be college a freshman. I was ready for whatever Southern University had for me.

After my first two weeks as a freshman, my roommate asked me if I could be her campaign manager because she was running for Miss Freshman. I had no idea what she was talking about; I was just happy that my roommate wanted to talk to me! Little did I know that this would be my first introduction to HBCU royalty and HBCU campaigning. I agreed to be her campaign manager and the fun began.

I watched my roommate study for weeks for the SGA test and prayed that she passed. Unlike some other HBCUs, Southern

University is one of the only HBCUs that requires you to pass the SGA test. This test challenges your knowledge of the organization and its structure. To campaign for any SGA position, you must pass this test. Talk about anxiety.

My roommate passed the test and, the very next day, we got to work planning and prepping her campaign. We dorm raided and passed out T-shirts to support her at the Freshman Revue. She won her election! And I continued to support her throughout her reign, doing her makeup for games and appearances. It was a fast-paced life but glamorous.

The following year, I became a campus photographer, an on-campus make-up artist, and a live painter at the local night scene. I explored all of my talents and found myself. I joined C100 Black Women of Southern University, where I found some of my best friends. After three years of a lot of travel and experiences, I felt that my college experience wouldn't be complete until I got involved in student leadership. Honestly, student leadership was intimidating; the body itself seemed so serious. But I decided that I wanted to go big or go home. I wanted to run for Miss

Southern University and A & M College. I had no idea what was ahead of me. As previously mentioned, the SGA test is the gatekeeper of all student elections. Until 2017, any female student with the right amount of credit hours and the right GPA could run for Miss Southern University, should she pass the SGA test. I decided over the Thanksgiving and Christmas breaks that I was going to commit to running. During the break, I read on social media that the SGA Senate was passing a new amendment that anyone running for a top-tier position would need one year of SGA experience in addition to the credit hour and GPA requirements. This meant that I was no longer eligible to run for Miss Southern University because I had never been in SGA before.

I decided that since I was no longer eligible to run for Miss Southern, I would get my one year of SGA experience. I was going to run for Miss Southern University one way or another. I had to retake a class that was only offered in the spring, so my expected graduation date was extended. That also meant that I would be enrolled for another election season. Without any experience in SGA, I was still eligible to run for Miss Senior. In hindsight, I was so fearless and so determined and so confident. No one in my family had ever embarked on anything like I was, at Southern. I passed my first SGA test and was ready to prepare for my campaign.

Because I didn't have much money for campaigning, I had to get creative. I created the graphics for my campaign materials. My photography team offered to take my photos. My classmates and friends made up my campaign team. My theme was "The Perfect Shot." As a marketing major, I knew the best way to market myself would be through photography. Everyone knew me as "the camera girl" on campus. Being an on-campus photographer allowed me to network with so many people on campus. That was going to set me apart from everyone else. I gave the campaign my very best; I met so many people and I truly enjoyed the experience. The results were announced, and I won!

The entire world of HBCU royalty was new to me. I was so eager to soak everything in. My first time representing as a queen was at the NASAP 2019 Conference, at Savannah State University in Savannah Georgia. It was a week-long experience of networking, fellowship, and leadership training for HBCU student leaders from around the country. Everyone was trying to get to know as many people as they could, so naturally, we took to social media. I documented my experience through selfies and videos on Instagram. Towards the end of the conference, Instagram account "@HBCUPrideNation," found my pictures on Instagram. All it took was one repost, and I went viral! I ended up making a big network from this one moment. Things don't just happen by chance; they're meant to be. I left the conference so fulfilled, I truly felt that I was walking in my purpose. I went into my reign as Miss Senior focused and driven. I would soon understand the saying "Heavy is the Head that wears the crown".

This reign was the hardest year of my college life. It was truly a test of my strength, endurance, and perseverance in the face of opposition. I learned so much about myself. I learned that I was so strong, no one could deter me from anything that I had already put my mind to. I learned that there will be times that your light shines so brightly that others can't see their own. I learned that regardless of others not being able to see their light, mine would continue to shine bright. I embodied Isaiah 54:17 and told myself, "He never said the weapons wouldn't form; He said they wouldn't prosper." Through all of the adversity I faced in this one year, I gained so much and built meaningful relationships in my community.

During this reign, my court was blessed with a hair sponsor. In exchange for social media marketing, we received free hair. This was the first time in my life I ever wore a wig. I was rocking a short Nia Long cut, but I knew I would need to look the part and glad to do so. I appreciated the protection it provided for my hair to maintain throughout the football season. I've always done my hair, skin, and nails. This experience was the glitz and glamour.

Then, I began my journey as an influencer. I got my first college job during my reign. I worked in our hair sponsor's boutique. My queen schedule didn't allow for regular working hours, but the boutique gave me the flexibility to work while being a full-time student and being a queen.

While being an influencer and working, I learned a lot about business and the marketing power I had as an influencer. I already had a background in photography, and I was studying marketing in school. The rest just fell in place. It was the best job That I could have had in school. Through my influence with the hair store, I gained more business opportunities and relationships with other black-owned businesses. From there, I ventured into opportunities with bigger brands in companies varying from fashion to makeup and clothing.

Through my local relationships, I was able to meet all kinds of people including radio personality and comedian Rickey Smiley. I was invited to have lunch with Rickey Smiley at a local restaurant. When I got the invite, I ran into my room and changed into a casual skirt suit, and heels. My training as a queen was so important to the moments that were just ahead of me. I used to give my advisor grief for being critical of the small details of our appearances as queens, but I am forever thankful for her guidance. The world will always be critical of us, but we can give the world our best presentation.

When I showed up at the restaurant, I soon realized that I was the youngest person in the room. And not only was I the youngest but one of three females. All eyes are on me. I was in a room filled with doctors and lawyers, friends of Rickey Smiley, and honorable city officials. I was quiet for most of the lunch, just observing and listening. I was just so humbled to be in the same space.

Towards the end of the lunch, Rickey Smiley passed by me. After talking with him, he was so impressed by me, he thought I was one of the restaurant's owners. I told to him that I was just a college student and a class queen. He returned to the table to share with the other guests who I was. I had to be twenty-one at the time. Rickey invited me into the conversation and began to tell me how much he appreciated my mannerisms, self-awareness, and overall presentation. Just from sitting quietly at a lunch, I gained a mentor of a lifetime.

Later that evening, I went to his book signing and exchanged contacts with Rickey, not knowing just how large this relationship would benefit me in the future. He kept up with me on social media, always leaving comments of encouragement and support. Influencing had a huge impact on my reign.

By the end of my reign at the 2019 Bayou Classic, I had the opportunity to be the first live stream host of the Bayou Classic Battle of the Bands. This opportunity was once in a lifetime. Live streaming the Battle had never been done before, and it was the experience of a lifetime! I was a photographer and media intern for the Bayou Classic years prior, but that was nothing compared to this hosting opportunity.

By the end of this Bayou Classic weekend, I decided that I was going to run for Miss Southern University. Over the Christmas break, I racked my brain for a campaign theme that would be timeless, elegant, and a true representation of how I saw myself.

I narrowed my theme down to 007, a classic James Bond concept, but I wanted to highlight the lineage of Miss Southern University. So, I changed the numbers to 088 to represent being the 88th Miss Southern University. The number 88 has become such a symbol in my life. It reminds me of how much I've overcome and accomplished. With the money that I saved working at the hair boutique, along with supportive sponsors, I began planning my campaign. At that point, my purpose to be Miss Southern came full circle because I had the guidance of the very first Miss Southern, I saw during my freshman orientation. I will always have love for my 84th. I can't even put into words how much she truly inspired me.

The spring semester came around, and I passed the SGA test yet again. I was prepared for nothing but success. This one was personal. I had already proven to myself that I was capable, but this time I had a point to prove. So many people doubted me and wanted to see me fail. But nothing can stop what God has already destined to be.

This campaign season was a turning point in HBCU campaigning. This was the year of social media. Through my networking from the NASAP conferences I had attended in the two summers prior, I noticed other HBCU Royals sending and posting endorsement videos on my behalf, addressing to my student body!

As my campaign week unfolded, more support was posted. I couldn't believe that my personal goal with now an urgent project for such a larger-than-life person. Rickey wanted to support me in any way he could. There wasn't much that I could tell him because only our student body could vote. But he found a way to express his support.

On the morning of election day, Rickey DM'd (direct messaged) me, telling me to listen to his morning show. I spent the night in my mom's hotel room, so I turned on the radio on the alarm clock. Rickey Smiley was raving about how we met, how much of a positive representation I was to the community and what a role model I was for young women. This was the most controversial moment in HBCU campaign history.

A celebrity endorsement of this size had never happened before. Everyone across America knew who I was and what I was trying to achieve. Rickey Smiley dedicated his entire morning show to telling people to vote me as Miss Southern University. I remember listening with my jaw dropped, watching my mom cry tears of extreme joy. Before I could catch my breath, he spelled out my Instagram handle, letter for letter. By the time he got to the last letter, my Instagram account blew up. I jumped from 7000 followers to 14,000 in four minutes. I received messages asking me to speak on panels, to model clothes and attend events across the country. I started getting messages from local radio listeners, sharing videos of Rickey talking about me on the radio from their cars. After ten minutes of the fast influx of notifications, my Instagram shut down.

In the midst of my celebration, I received a call from the election commission stating that I was being sanctioned for the day because candidates cannot campaign on the radio. Keep in mind, this was the last day of campaign week and a vital day to encourage students to vote. I knew I didn't personally or intentionally decide to campaign on the radio. That was solely the decision of someone else. However, I followed the rules of the elections commission I stopped all of my campaigning across the campus. And I prayed. As devastating as this news was, I remained calm and collected. My spirit told me everything was going to be okay.

I waited the day out until election results were announced. My mom and I continue to pray and updated Ricky Smiley with the news. He graciously brought me comfort on the phone, as we waited. He told me how proud of me he was and expressed to my mom how proud she should be. He talked on the phone with us while we awaited the election results.

The results came back, and I'd won by a landslide, 892:622. Throughout the entire campaign, I had never been so focused. My purpose was so clear to me. I had accomplished something that as a freshman, I never even dreamed of. I remained true to myself and true to my peers. And the genuine relationships that I had with them carried me through to victory.

My reign was a dream; although it was full of adventure and life lessons, I had the best advisor I could have asked for. She lifted me up, she comforted me, and she pushed me when things got tough. Just before my reign began, I lost two of my advisors to new job opportunities at another HBCU, but even from far away, they were such great supporters and actively assisted me throughout my reign.

One of the people nearest to my heart and one of my favorite Southernite, Anthony Kenney, was my SGA President and escort. He supported me through every trial throughout my reign and became one of my closest friends and still my partner in crime to this day. Love you, Kenney!

Some of my fondest memories from my Miss Southern reign include the making of my coronation gown. My best friend's mom is a designer. She sketched and created my custom gown and cape.

The experience meant so much to me, as this woman was like my second mother. My coronation was so dear to me, my twin brothers (I'm a triplet) presented me at my coronation as a surprise. After a week of praying that my advisors who left at the beginning of my reign would be able to attend coronation. Sadly, they told me that they couldn't make it, and I was heartbroken!

Just to surprise me at my coronation, bearing beautiful gifts and a beautiful dance presentation that brought me to tears.

One year of being Miss Southern changed my life. But every Miss Southern knows that you will forever be someone's Miss Southern. The impact I had on my community and communities around the country will always remind me of my strength, my truth, and my purpose.

I encourage anyone who wants to pursue their wildest dreams to first know yourself, and your purpose will be made clear to you. Focus on your growth, be kind to yourself and others and never quit. Your dreams are only one affirmation away. Speak greatness into your life every day. Manifest your wildest dreams, and one day they'll come true.

Royally,
The 88th Miss Southern University and A&M College

About Darby Smith

Darby Smith is a native of Shreveport, Louisiana and a proud two time graduate of Southern University and A&M College. Darby earned her Bachelors of Science in Business Marketing in the Spring of 2019. In May 2021, Darby earned her Master's degree in Public Administration. She is the daughter of Southern University graduates, has an older sister, Colby–who is also a Southern graduate, and is a triplet with identical brothers, Tyler and Morgan. She comes from a praying family and lives by Bible scripture, Isaiah 54:17; He said the weapons would form, but they will not prosper.

Highly involved on campus, Darby was a photographer on the Human Jukebox Media Team (2016-2018) and DaEdge1 Productions (2015-2017), was a member of Collegiate 100 Women and SU Volunteers, and served as the 2017-2018 Miss Senior. In 2017, Darby was the first intern and live streaming host for the Bayou Classic Battle of the Bands with ONYX Television Network based in Shreveport, LA. In the Spring of 2018, Darby was elected as the 88th Miss Southern University and A & M College. Her election gained the support of Rickey Smiley of the Rickey Smiley Morning Show. Throughout her reign, Darby coordinated fundraising events for St. Jude's Foundation, including the continuation of the Little Miss SU Pageant.

Darby is currently the Director of Student Activities and Leadership Development at Wiley College, in Marshall, Texas– Home of the Great Debaters. She enjoys enriching her students' HBCU experience through mentoring, advising The Wiley College Royal Court, and supporting student development in leadership skills as upstanding citizens of their society and educated leaders of their communities.

Darby stays connected in the HBCU community through brand ambassadorships with HBCU Pride Nation and Support Black Colleges. In her free time, she runs a online vintage apparel boutique, The Co. You Keep whole creating Social Media Content in the fashion and beauty industry.

According to RP Podcast
CEO/Founder: Ritha Pierre, Esq.
@accordingtorp
accordingtorp@gmail.com

ACTIVate
CEO/Founder: Yladera Drummond, J.D.
contact@activateleadership.org
info@yladeradrummond.com
www.yladeradrummond.com
www.activateleadership.org

AC Events
The Luxury Planning Experience
CEO/Founder: Amy Agbottah
amy@amycynthiaevents.com

Allen Financial Solutions

CEO/Founder: Jay Allen

@jay83allen

@Jay Allen

allen.jonathan83@gmail.com

The Ancestor Key

CEO/Founder: Ja'el Gordon

504-356-1466

theancestor@gmail.com

The Alli Group, LLC
Real Estate Management

Founders: Lawrence & Nickia Alli

@thealligroupllc

nickia.alli@gmail.com

www.thealligroupllc.com

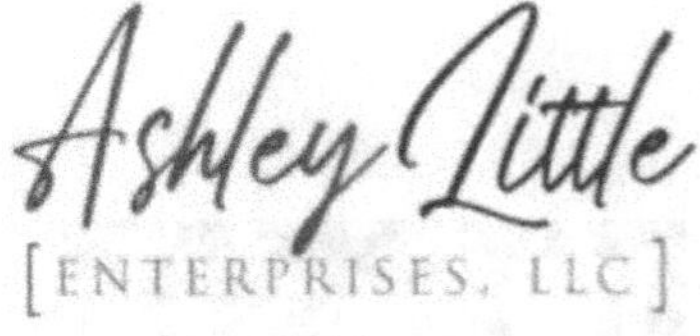

Ashley Little Enterprises, LLC

CEO/Founder: Dr. Ashley Little

@_ashleyalittle

@Ashley Little

aalittle08@gmail.com

www.ashleylittleenterprises.com

AMMEA

President: Ernest Stackhouse

ej.stackhouse@gmail.com

www.ammea.org

Assurance Tax & Accounting Group, LLC
CEO/Founder:
Kimberlee Collins-Walker
8676 Goodwood Blvd., Ste. 102
Baton Rouge, LA 70876
225-757-7518
kim@assurancetaxbr.com
www.assurancetaxbr.com

Baker & Baker Realty, LLC
CEO/Founder: Christopher Baker
@seedougieblake
@Christopher D. Baker
baker.christopher@gmail.com

The Black Techies/Podcast
CEO/Founder: Herbert L. Seward, III
Where black culture meets the world of technology.
www.theblacktechies.com

BLKWOMENHUSTLE
CEO/Founder: Lashawn Dreher
@blkwomenhustle
@Blk Women Hustle
info@blkwomenhustle.com

Block Band Music & Publishing, LLC
CEO/Founder: D. Rashad Watters
919-698-2560
blockbandmusic@gmail.com

Boardroom Brand, LLC
CEO/Founder: Samuel Brown, III
@_gxxdy
samuel.brown.three@gmail.com

Bound By Conscious Concepts

CEO/Founder: Kathryn Lomax

@msklovibes223

@Klo-Kathryn Lomax

972-638-9823

klomax@bbconcepts.com

Brooks Art Collective

CEO/Founder: LaToya Brooks

@brooksartcollective

@brooksartcollective

brooksartcollective@gmail.com

Campaign Engineers

Campaign Engineers

CEO/Founder: Chris Smith

@csmithatl

csmithl911@gmail.com

Chef Batts

CEO/Founder: Keith Batts

@chefbatts

booking@chefbatts.com

Cici's Freelance Services

CEO/Founder:
Courtney "Cici" Walker, MPA

○ @cicisfreelanceservices

☎ 225-288-8216

✉ cicisfreelanceservices@gmail.com

DD Jones Enterprise

CEO/Founder: Darcele Jones-Horton

✉ darceleh@bellsouth.net

Deroune Services, LLC

CEO/Founder: Marina Zeno

☎ 337-418-0785

Eclectikread Marketing

CEO/Founder: Christa Newkirk

○ @chris_ta_da

✉ info@eclectikread.com

Enlightened Visions, Inc.

CEO/Founder: TaNisha Fordham

✉ tanisha.fordham@gmail.com

🌐 www.enlightenedvisions.org

February First

CEO/Founder: Cedric Livingston

Director/Writer: *February First: A Stride Towards Freedom*

🌐 www.februaryfirstmovie.com

Freeda's World Podcast

CEO/Founder: Ritha Pierre, Esq.

- @freedas_world
- accordingtorp@gmail.com

Harbor Institute

CEO/Founder:

Rasheed Ali Cromwell, J.D.

- @theharborinstitute
- @The Harbor Institute
- @harborinstitute
- racromwell@theharborinstitute.com

HBCU 101

CEO/Founder: Jahliel Thurman

- @HBCU101
- jahlielthurman@gmail.com
- www.hbcu101.com

The HBCU Band Experience with Christy Walker

CEO/Founder: Dr. Christy Walker

- christywalker57@gmail.com
- www.christywalker.com

HBCU Buzz

(HBCU Buzz | Taper, Inc. | Root Care Health)

CEO/Founder: Luke Lawal, Jr.

- @lukelawal
- @L & COMPANY
- 301-221-1719
- lawal@lcompany.co

HBCU Cheer Black Excellence

- @HBCUcheer
- HBCUcheerleaders@yahoo.com

The HBCU Experience Movement, LLC

CEO/Founder: Dr. Ashley Little

@ @_ashleyalittle

@DrAshley Little

thehbcuexperiencemovement@gmail.com

www.thehbcuexperiencemovement.com

HBCU Grad

CEO/Founder: Todd Finley

312-535-8511

www.hbcugraduates.com

HBCU Girls Talk

CEO/Founder: TeeCee Camper

@HBCUgirlstalk

talkgirls@yahoo.com

HBCU Pride Nation

CEO/Founder: Travis Jackson

@HBCUpridenation

@HBCU Pride Nation

travispjackson@gmail.com

HBCU Pulse

CEO/Founder: Randall Barnes

@HBCUpulse

@thehbcupulse

www.hbcupulse.com

HBCU Times

CEO/Founders: David Staten, Ph. &
Bridget Hollis Staten, Ph.D

📷 @HBCU_times8892

f @HBCU Times

✉ hbcutimes@gmail.com

HBCU Wall Street

CEO/Founders:
   Torrence Reed & Jamerus Peyton

f @HBCU Wall Street

✉ info@hbcuwallstreet.com

H.E.R. Story Podcast

H.E.R. Story with J. Jamison
CEO/Founder: Janea Jamison

📷 @herstory _podcast

#Herstorymovement

Holistic Practitioners

CEO/Founder: Tianna Bynum

f @Tianna Bynum

✉ tpb33@georgetown.edu

ICG Marriage & Family Therapy

CEO/Founders:
   Jabari & Stephanie Walthour

📷 @thedopesextherapist

✉ stephanie@intimacycenterga.com

www www.intimacycenterga.com

Johnson Capital

CEO/Founder: Marcus Johnson

📷 @marcusdiontej

✉ marcus@johnsoncap.com

Journee Enterprises

CEO/Founder: Fred Whit

⊙ @frederickwjr

f @Fred Whit

✉ frederickwjr@yahoo.com

J.Robins CPA, LLC

CEO/Founder: Joseph Robins

⊙ @robinscpa

f @jrobinscpa

9800 Line Hwy., Ste. 261

Baton Rouge, LA 70816

☎ 225-650-7306

✉ info@jrobinscpa.com

🌐 www.jrobinscpa.com

Kelly Collaborative Medicine

CEO/Founder: Dr. Kathyrn Kelly

10801 Lockwood Dr., Ste. 160

Silver Spring, MD 20901

☎ 301-298-1040

🌐 www.kellymedicinemd.com

The Lady BUGS

CEO/Founder: Tatiana Tinsley Dorsey

⊙ @theladybugsoffical

f @HBCU Times

✉ ladybugs_HQ@googlegroups.com

LEMM Media Group

CEO/Founder: Cremel Nakia Burney

⊙ @cremel_the_creator

✉ cremelburney@gmail.com

Little Publishing, LLC
CEO/Founder: Dr. Ashley Little
@ @_ashleyalittle
f @DrAshley Little
✉ info@ashleyalittle.com
www www.ashleylittleenterprises.com

The Marching Force
700 Emancipation Dr.
Hampton, VA 23668
www www.supportthematchingforce.com

Swing Into Their Dreams Foundation
Co-Founders: Pamela Parker and
    Lynn Demmons
✉ swingintotheirdreams@gmail.com
www www.swingintotheirdreams.com

The Marching Podcast
CEO/Founder: Joseph Beard
✉ marchingpodcast@gmail.com
www www.themarchingpodcast.com

LK Productions
CEO/Founder: Larry King
@ @lk_rrproduction
f @Larry King
✉ lkproduction@yahoo.com

Marching Sport
CEO/Founder: Gerard Howard
✉ gerardhoward@gmail.com

Minority Cannabis Business Association

President: Shanita Penny

📷 @Minority Cannabis

f @MCBA.Org

🐦 @MinCannBusAssoc

in @Minority Cannabis Business Association

📟 202-681-2889

✉ info@minoritycannabis.org

www www.minoritycannabis.org

Mills Academy

CEO/Founder: Airneica Mills

📟 662-822-6976

✉ millsacademy1@gmail.com

MilRo Entertainment

CEO/Founder: Chevis Anderson

✉ milrosplace@yahoo.com

NC Dance District

CEO/Founder: Dr. Kellye Worth Hall

📷 @divadoc5

f @Kellye Worth Hall

✉ delta906@gmail.com

Never2Fly2Pray

CEO/Founder: Jeffrey Lee Sawyer

📷 @never2fly2pray

f @Jeffrey Lee

✉ htdogwtr@yahoo.com

NXLevel Travel (NXLTRVL)

CEO: Hercules Conway
@herc3k
@Hercules Conway
COO: Newton Dennis
@nxlevel
@Newton Dennis
info@nxleveltravel.com
www.nxleveltravel.com

The Phoenix Professional Network

CEO/Founder: DJavon Alston
@thephoenixnetwork757
@DJavon Alston
thephoenixnetwork757@gmail.com

OEDM Group

CEO/Principal Owner: Justin Blake
@oedmgroup.com
contact@oedmgroup.com
www.oedmgroup.com

PILAR

Co-Owner: Nate Perry
@barpilar
nate@pilardc.com

PacketStealer Gaming

CEO/Founder: David Matthews
packetstealer@outlook.com

Queen Series

CEO/Founder: Randall Barnes
aqueenseries@gmail.com

Reid Creative Solutions, LLC

CEO/Founder: Aja Reid

919-822-2892

info@reidcreativesolutions.com

www.reidcreativesolutions.com

Shani L., Relationship Enthusiast

CEO/Founder: Porscha Lee Taylor

@shanilrelationshipenthusiast

info@shanilfarmer.com

www.shanilfarmer.com

SayYes

Say Yes, LLC

CEO/Founder: Porscha Lee Taylor

@sayyesplanners

info@sayyescareer.com

www.sayyesplanners.com

She Is Magazine

CEO/Founder: Ciara Horton

@sheisemagazine

@Ciara Horton

ciarasheisemagazine.com

SC DJ WORM 803

CEO/Founder: Jamie Brunson

@SCDJWORM803

@SC DJ Worm 803

@SCDJWORM803

@SC DJ Worm 803

scdjworm803@gmail.com

www.scdjworm803.com

Southern University A&M College

801 Harding Blvd.

Baton Rouge, LA 70807

225-771-4500

Southern University Alumni Federation

124 Roosevelt Steptoe Dr.

Baton Rouge, LA 70807

225-771-4200

sualumni@sualumni.org

Success and Religion

CEO/Founder: Micheal Taylor

successismyreligion@gmail.com

Sugar Top Spirit & Beverage Co.

CEO/Founder: Terri White

@sugartopspirits

@sugartopspirits

tl.white412@gmail.com

www.sugartopspirits.com

SPGBK

Springbreak Watches (SPGBK)

CEO/Founder: Kwame Molden

@SPGBK

@Kwame Molden

info@springbreakwatches.com

Stamp'd Travel

CEO/Founder:

Jocelyn Hadrick Alexander

@jocehadyou

jocelyn.h.alexander@gmail.com

www.stampdtravel.com

SwagHer

Vice President of Sales / Marketing:

Jarmel Roberson

@swaghermagazine

jroberson@swagher.net

www.swagher.net

TLW Photography
CEO/Founder: Taylor Whitehead
mrknowitall91@aol.com

Uplift Clothing Apparel
CEO/Founder: Jermaine Simpson
@upliftclothingapparel
www.upliftclothingapparel.com

Upward Path
CEO/Founder:
Cameron Chamlers Dupree
@upwardpathtc
contact@upwardpathtc.com
www.upwardpathtc.com

The Urban Learning &
Leadership Center, Inc.

**The Urban Learning &
Leadership Center, Inc.**
President/Co-Founder:
John W. Hodge, Ed.D
jhodge@ulleschools.com

**The Vernon Group
Cooperative Solutions**
CEO/Founder: Anthony V. Stevens
@investednu
info@vernongroupllc.com

Vision Tree, LLC
CEO/Founder: Dr. Jorim Reed
@upwardpathtc
visiontreellc@gmail.com

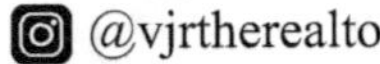

VJR Real Estate

CEO/Founder: Victor Collins, Jr.

@vjrtherealtor

vic@thevjrgroup.com

Yard Talk 101

CEO/Founder: Jahliel Thurman

@YardTalk101

www.yardtalk101.com

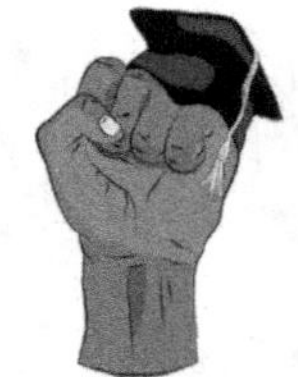

We Are Educated, Inc.

We Are Educated, Inc.

CEO/Founder: Ayanna Spivey

@ayannaceleste

ayanna.spivey@yahoo.com

Zoom Technologies, LLC

CEO/Founder: Torrence Reed

@torrencereed3

support@zoom-technologies.co

9 781734 931174